FIND YOU
FIND LOVE

Get to the heart of love and
relationships using EFT

WENDY FRY

AUTHOR'S DECLARATION

ISBN Number: 9781910202463

Author profile photography: Peter Kavanagh

Illustrator: Amy Branton

Orders:

You can order via www.amazon.co.uk

If you would like a signed copy of the book and a personalised dedication you can contact me personally via my website www.wendyfry.com

PRAISE FOR FIND YOU, FIND LOVE

"Wendy has written a highly accessible book that first enables you to turn inwards and experience more self-love and then take this out into the world in your relationships. Her Spotlight Process is a very practical solution to help you overcome your relationship challenges. This is a dynamic book that you will use time and time again, and each time you do, it will deepen your connection with yourself and others."

Sasha Allenby - Bestselling Author of Matrix Reimprinting Using EFT, Book Coach, Ghost Writer and Publishing CEO.

'' Many people find it hard to find love these days so Wendy's delightful book is perfect for helping people to clear deep rooted blocks and help them find their way to a happier and more loving future. The book is packed with brilliant exercises, case studies and Wendy's own fascinating story. It's a must have on every book shelf. I love this book''

Anne Jirsch - Bestselling Author of Instant Intuition, The Future is Yours, Cosmic Energy, Create Your Perfect Future.

"Find YOU, Find LOVE is a workbook leading the reader to resolve and heal themselves through insights discovered using The Spotlight Process and EFT. The reader is presented with clear, concise guidance on how to use the book and how to work through the exercises. The Spotlight Process combines physical with psychological processing via meta positioning in an interesting new effective approach. Also, the many case studies elucidate the methods used"

Curly Martin - Bestselling Author of The Life Coaching Handbook, The Business Coaching Handbook and The Personal Success Handbook.

''Find YOU, Find LOVE by Wendy Fry takes you lovingly by the hand and guides you on a powerful journey to heal your past relationships, transforming your past where you have experienced separation, not feeling safe in the world and unloved. Lovingly guiding you to open your heart once again, to love and be loved. Every relationship we have offers us an opportunity to heal and the

Introduction

Find YOU
Find LOVE

Welcome aboard what will be an enlightening adventure for you-this will be a journey like no other! I want to reassure you that whatever love and relationship challenges you are facing that help is indeed here for you. Whatever 'stuckness' you might feel, whatever fears about the future this book will be the guiding light that shines new hope on love and relationships.

This isn't just a 'read me book'. It is designed to gently challenge you to be really honest with yourself, so that you can get down to the bare bones of finding love.

You will be asked plenty of thought provoking questions that will expand your thinking, enabling you to grow beyond your wildest dreams. You will be expertly guided to use the tried and tested methods that will take you to the heart of love and relationships.

Find YOU, Find LOVE includes the following tools and transformational techniques:

   • **EFT Process**

   • **Insightful Questions**

   • **Practical Exercises**

   • **The Spotlight Process**

   • **Heart Based Exercises**

- **Power Questions**

- **Audio Downloads**

Find You Find Love not only helps you to be the best you can be, it will act as your personal resource guide, teaching you step by step how to get out of your own way, so that you can experience the love that you truly deserve.

Some commitment will be required from you and a willingness to learn about yourself, your past, your beliefs and perceptions about love and relationships and in doing so, this will open up for you a whole new world of opportunity.

Here are just some of the insightful things you gain from applying the transformational techniques that you will discover in Find YOU, Find LOVE

- **Explore your thinking and how this may be limiting you**
- **Expose the inner critic that holds you back and gets in your way of achieving your love and relationship goals**
- **Identify and release limiting core beliefs and any aspects of the past that may be holding you back from achieving the love and relationships you desire**
- **Discover the connection between your mind, body and emotions bringing all three into balance**
- **Learn how to align your thinking to that which you want for your future**
- **Find out how to shift patterns from the past to change your focus and change your life, love and relationships**
- **Master effective 'self questioning' techniques that guide you to awaken your heart and open the door to happiness**
- **Accept, love and appreciate yourself for who you are**
- **Get to the heart of love and relationships using EFT**

Operating from a place of possibility, taking time to reflect and work through any experiences that may have limited you, you will be able to turn those setbacks into the guiding steps that will lead you to happiness and fulfilment giving you renewed focus and clarity about what you want in terms of love and relationships.

THE SPOTLIGHT PROCESS -
SHINING THE LIGHT ON LOVE AND RELATIONSHIPS

With many years experience working as an Emotional Health and Relationship Consultant, guiding others to work through the reasons they have felt unloved, unappreciated and rejected, I have gone on to develop The Spotlight Process so that you too can find your way out of the clouds and into the light.

The Spotlight Process reviews your past, present and future and examines the events, perceptions and beliefs that may have contributed to your love and relation-ship problems up to now. You will gain awareness that the past need not influence the future, giving you the freedom, encouragement and motivation to start your journey of personal transformation and bring you back home to you, the place where love resides.

Together, we will work through any doubts you may have, transforming those doubts into stepping stones leading towards the future you desire, a future where you can be the 'real you' knowing that you are worthy and deserving of love.

You will learn how to let go of any limitations with courage, allowing you the freedom of mind to create your life exactly as you would like it to be.

- **Have you ever found yourself questioning why love seems so unattain-able?**
- **Have you ever wondered what you might be doing wrong and why love seems to be just beyond your reach?**
- **Have you ever felt that love will never find you or that you are somehow invisible when it comes to love?**

Using the tried and tested exercises throughout this book you will move from a place of hopelessness to happiness, from a sense of lack to a sense of love, from debilitating doubt to delightful daring. You will begin transforming unwanted emo-tions and overcome misconceptions about yourself and your lovability to become the person you have always been and just forgot about.

The insights that you will learn about yourself, the internal shifts you will make in your thinking will be the guiding light that brings you back home to you, a place where you will find the love you have been searching for.

MY STORY

I wrote this book for you as I have known within the deepest darkest parts of myself what it's like to feel unloved, lonely and hopeless both in and out of relationships. My first experience of believing I was unloved came when my dad left at the age of twelve. Now, as an adult I understand why he left though it was devastating and the beliefs that I formed impacted many of my relationships until I reached my thirties.

The emotional overwhelm that I experienced at that time was huge; it felt wrong for me to communicate what I was feeling. My mum talked about taking her own life and I felt huge responsibility to keep her safe from taking an overdose and to put her needs before my own. It felt unsafe for me to speak up about my own feelings for fear of upsetting any of my family and triggering their own guilt, loss and confusion. The personal rejection I felt was huge I had nowhere to go and no one to turn to, so I turned inside and shut the door on 'Me'.

I moved around a lot between the age of twelve and twenty three, living with different family members and also renting rooms in house shares. For most of that time I went through life feeling like a spare part, unwanted and in the way. I was fed up with boxing up my life and trying to find a place which I could call home. I felt restless with no sense of belonging, purpose or wholeness.

My Nan died when I was twenty three and I felt even more isolated, we had been very close as I had spent some of my teenage years living with her. It seemed like nobody really understood me and that my thoughts and feelings didn't matter so I kept everything inside

In my late twenties I was diagnosed with depression and suffered anxiety, panic attacks and had low self esteem. My mum had taught me indirectly to think that suicide might be a way out of the emptiness I felt inside. I contemplated this and got as far as buying pills and booze, though I never actually took the overdose - something stopped me. Perhaps it was the forgotten part of me that was speaking up very quietly for the first time, the 'me' that wanted to be loved, heard and appreciated.

Have you been in that place yourself - hovering between wanting to live and wanting to die, or know someone who has?

From the age of fifteen, I was reckless in terms of my behaviour, seeking love in the arms of others but not realising until I was thirty that I was doing so by the wrong means. It was a confusing time and as a twelve year old I formed the belief that I had to give myself physically in order to be loved. I had misunderstood my dad's communications about intimacy, love and relationships and it was a huge learning curve to realise that giving myself physically before building a relationship and getting to know someone as a person was not a guarantee that I would be loved or that a relationship would last.

I had been walking around in a daze and seeking out people who confirmed my lack of love, self worth and respect. I felt easily discarded, further compounding my belief that I was worthless and unlovable. I had been on auto-pilot for way too long operating from a belief that wasn't true.

From personal experience, I know what it is like to be in that pit of despair that some call 'the dark night of the soul' and all that it entails, I realised I had a choice to either stay trapped in a living nightmare, or find a way to move on from the prison I had created in my mind.

I reach out from my heart to yours through the contents of this book in the hope that I can support you in making a choice to start your life afresh and to let you know that you are not alone.

I will be your guiding light on your journey of transformation. It is the choices you make from now on that will ultimately lift you up or keep you down.

GET TO THE HEART OF LOVE

- **Are you ready for your transformational journey, a journey of self discovery?**

- **Are you willing to step up, take action and trust yourself enough to know that now is the perfect time to make positive and lasting changes in your life?**

- **Are you ready to transform the past using your experiences to work for you and not against you?**

- **Do you want to make decisions that allow you to be who you really are and make choices that serve you, leading you to reach your full potential?**

- **Are you ready for love, love that fills you up completely, love that is meaningful, lasting and satisfying?**

Fasten your seat belt, brace yourself, take a nice deep and easy breath and know that from this moment on, I will be beside you every step of the way on the journey back home to you.

You are in safe hands so let the ride commence, and you can be secure in the knowledge that not only will this book clarify what's been stopping you from finding the love you want up to now, it will also show you how to move beyond a place of uncertainty and fear so that you need never look back for a single second.

You may not realise it yet, but the best is yet to come!

HOW TO USE THIS BOOK TO TRANSFORM YOUR LIFE AND LOVE RELATIONSHIPS

This book has been structured for you to work through at your own pace. The book's flexibility means it is possible to work through all of the exercises systematically, or dip in and out, choosing the ones that you are drawn to first and starting with those. There may be exercises that you intuitively know you would benefit from spending a little more time on or revisiting again at a later date as the book can be used time and time again to resolve love and relationship difficulties.

You can work through the book on your own, or perhaps planning a day or two with a friend to support each other through a series of exercises. If you feel that you would benefit from a personal support programme with me please do make contact.

MAKING SOME 'YOU TIME'

I do recommend that you plan ahead and commit to prioritising some 'you time' and make dates with yourself to complete the processes that will lead to personal transformation. Making time for yourself will be one of the best investments you have ever made. Self care will ultimately lead to self love.

The contents of this book will offer you a tool kit of exercises The EFT Process, The Spotlight Process, Insightful Questions, Practical Exercises, Heart Based Exercises and Power Questions that will guide you through any current challenges or problems from the past that may have been lingering around and kicking up a stink.

I can speak with authority about the effectiveness of the exercises, having completed and worked through them many times myself also using the same tools and techniques with my clients.

The book will stimulate you by asking questions to get to the heart of love and relationships. It will inspire you to explore and uncover your limiting beliefs and blocks that have been holding you back from feeling more loving and lovable, teaching you the tricks of the trade to improve your confidence in any relationship.

Working through the book, you will gain many personal insights, understand yourself better and find the ability to resolve and heal old wounds. The techniques will support you to move on from the past and give you a clearer sense of who you are and where you are headed.

TAKING THE TIME YOU NEED TO AND BEING PATIENT WITH YOURSELF

Be patient and kind to yourself as you read and work through this book, knowing it will ultimately lead to your personal transformation.

If you feel that you would like support, perhaps buddy up with a friend to work through the book with you.   Alternatively, do contact me if you wish me to work with me privately.

I suggest that you purchase a journal or notebook that you can use alongside Find YOU, Find LOVE, where you can record your thoughts, feelings and emotions as you move through the aspects of your love and relationship challenges.   It will be helpful to record and document your progress as you go along.

Giving you the tools to master your emotions and steer the way ahead, Find YOU, Find LOVE will support you in changing your beliefs and changing your life.

My website **www.wendyfry.com**   offers downloadable resources and additional information that you may find useful.

Your task is not to seek for love, but merely to seek and find all the barriers within yourself that you have built against it - Rumi

Chapter 1

Get to the Heart of Love and Relationships Using EFT

THE EMOTIONAL FREEDOM TECHNIQUE

I really do feel that EFT deserves a drum roll of introduction, appreciation and acknowledgement, as using it may seriously improve your emotional wellbeing and in turn your relationships and that, wouldn't you agree, is worth a drum roll or three?

I don't know anyone who doesn't want to be free from unwanted negative emotions or who doesn't want to improve their love and relationships or their ability to love and be loved. There is great freedom and personal transformation that comes from using this technique and you will experience that for yourself if you follow the guidelines offered to you.

I'm hopeful that once you have learnt and applied EFT to the areas of your life you wish to work on, EFT will become as regular for you as brushing your teeth. EFT can be compared to daily brushing to balance energy. It can be used as 'first aid' and applied as and when needed in the moment. It can also be used for long term healing and will certainly be less painful than a root canal. When you are able to work on the root of a problem, smaller, related problems will no longer influence you to such a great effect.

EFT has the potential to change your beliefs and in turn transform your life. You will find your life improving either in subtle ways or with dramatic effect depending on how often you apply the technique. When you free yourself from past hurts and fears, clearing emotional baggage easily and quickly, you break old patterns and behaviours and open up for yourself a world full of love and opportunity.

EFT AND THE RIPPLE EFFECT

Many people find that using EFT on one problem, in fact resolves other problems at the same time. As our energy shifts and changes and begins flowing freely, so our thoughts, feelings and emotions shift and change. Life starts to look rosy again.

EFT has a ripple effect, just like casting a pebble into a still lake, the ripples of change spread out into all areas of your life. Every ripple, every thought, every feeling, every word and every action you cast out will create and bring to you amazing life changes.

I use EFT every day. I recommend you, too, use EFT as part of your natural daily health plan to support you in balancing your emotional health and wellbeing.

Take a moment to reflect and consider these questions carefully:

- **Do you want to be free from emotional ties to the past?**
- **Free from fear and worry?**

- **Free from emotional baggage that may have been weighting you down?**
- **Do you want to feel more hopeful about the future?**
- **More confident?**
- **More loving?**
- **Do you want to live a life of joy and feel optimistic about the future?**

EFT will support you in achieving this and more.

Are you in?

THE HISTORY OF GARY CRAIG 'THE MAIN MAN'

Gary Craig, founder of The Emotional Freedom Technique (EFT), is a very wise man. Gary suggests with EFT to "try it on everything" and I couldn't agree more. In my mind, EFT is the perfect remedy to be included in everyone's 'medicine cupboard' and the good news is that it has no nasty side effects!

Gary created EFT, The Emotional Freedom Technique as an offshoot from Roger Callahan's Thought Field Therapy (TFT). Gary simplified the process of TFT and created EFT. Gary understood that "the cause of all negative emotions is a disruption in the body's energy system" and he's used it with thousands of people to improve their physical and emotional health. What a legacy to leave behind, to be able to change lives for the better, using this simple technique

I came across the emotional freedom technique many years ago when I worked for a health care provider. Several of the therapists who were part of our network of affiliates, used EFT with their clients which had some very beneficial effects.

I became interested in this type of energy work, already being a qualified Reiki practitioner the concept appealed to me. As I gleaned more information about this powerful technique, I wanted to learn this not only for myself but also to share with my own clients.

I have personally used EFT to work through painful childhood memories, personal limitations and beliefs and I share this technique with my clients and now you the reader to support you in working through your own challenges and setbacks. EFT gives you the opportunity to transform and to be free from the ties that may have been binding you and keeping you stuck in the past.

WHAT IS EFT AND HOW CAN I USE IT?

EFT is classed as an Energy Psychology. Energy Psychology focuses on the connected relationship of energy, emotions, behaviours and health. EFT works by shifting the brain's electrochemistry and works by stimulating energy points on the surface of the skin.

EFT combines the principles of Chinese Medicine with modern psychology. Our emotional and physical health depends upon the smooth flow of energy through our body's energy meridians. Emotions affect our energy systems and when we are tuned into a negative thought, emotion, situation or event our energy system disrupts and literally responds to the thought.

IMPROVING ENERGY FLOW

By clearing and releasing emotional conflicts through EFT tapping, our energy system is stimulated and balances out any energy disruptions. Our energy flow is improved, in turn our physical health and emotional wellbeing is also improved.

EFT works in a similar way to acupuncture though without the use of needles to stimulate energy flow. EFT includes bringing awareness to emotional issues as well as physical ailments.

An acupuncturist would study more than three hundred meridian points and use a needle to stimulate energy flow. With EFT, we use our fingertips to tap gently on some of our energy meridian points/energy pathways to stimulate energy flow, transforming and releasing emotional and physical symptoms as we go.

We tap directly on the surface of the specific points with light and gentle tapping movements, some people may prefer to gently rub these spots if they are using EFT in a public space. Tapping gently and stimulating these points moves the flow of energy through the entire meridian system.

Once EFT has been learnt (and it's so easy to pick up) it can be used anywhere in any circumstance, it's portable and very easy to master and can often reduce an emotional intensity in as little as five to ten minutes of tapping. For some longer standing problems, several sessions and rounds of tapping may be required to reduce the emotional intensity.

There is great freedom in tapping and releasing your trapped or uneven energy flow, which has been blocked and holding you back from being open to love and loving relationships. Persist with using EFT regularly and you will reap the benefits tenfold.

Your energy can be influenced positively or negatively by what you think about. EFT will support you in dissolving and resolving the emotional charge connected to any memory, event or person. You can further help yourself by bringing your thinking into alignment and being aware of where your mind has been.

EFT can be applied to a range of emotional problems or physical symptoms. Once you are familiar with the technique, it will support you in not only releasing negative emotions, but will also allow you to tap into those inner resources you always had but just forgot about.

EFT can be used to clear past traumas, overwhelming emotions and can also be used to increase relaxation, happiness and joy. EFT can also be in the moment as and when a shock may occur.

It can be used to transform fears, anxieties, past events, current challenges, up-sets, disagreements, physical ailments, emotional problems, relationship problems, aiding personal healing, as well as self development, confidence building and life transformation – phew - and that's not all!

EFT has changed my life so much for the better and my hope is that it will change yours, in ways you never imagined possible. EFT has paved the way for me to the road of freedom and amazing opportunities and I share it here with you so that you can take your own journey to all that is possible.

I hope that after reading this book you will continue to use EFT in your everyday life. EFT is a technique I wish everyone knows about. It's so effective on many different levels. It can be used to manage day to day life, along with those unexpected things and it may also improve your physical health and emotional wellbeing, as well as deal with past or current challenges and setbacks.

It is my wish for you, that EFT transforms your life in the way it has transformed mine and the lives of the people I have shared this valuable resource with.

WHAT THE PEOPLE AT THE TOP ARE SAYING ABOUT EFT

Many self help authors, gurus and teachers endorse EFT, the word is waking up to the positive changes EFT brings and is spreading.

Louise L Hay author of You Can Heal Your Life said '' When I first heard about using tapping or EFT (Emotional freedom Technique), I thought it was delightful that something this simple and easy could really work''.

Dr Wayne Dyer recently said ''put away your scepticism, this really works...I've had great results with tapping in my own life.''

Jack Canfield, Co-creator of Chicken Soup for the Soul, calls it ''the most powerful new transformational technology to come along in years.''

If you wish to research EFT further, there are free tutorials on Gary Craigs website

www.emofree.com the focus of this book is to teach you to use EFT as a basic technique for clearing the past.

I had the privilege of training as an Advanced EFT and Matrix Reimprinting Practitioner with the wonderful Karl Dawson **www.efttrainingcourses.net** Karl co-authors Matrix Reimprinting Using EFT with Sasha Allenby, his latest book Transform Your Beliefs, Transform Your Life co-authored with Kate Marillat are both excellent reads if you wish to develop your EFT and love and relationship toolkit.

Your mind and body react to a continuous flow of information coming in through your senses. Every thought you think affects your body (physiology) and emotions. Likewise every physical action affects your thinking and your mood. Thoughts can create and heighten stress, sadness, depression as well as intensify feelings of joy, happiness and love.

I wish to encourage you to be aware from this moment on how your mind-body connection works. Being aware of this connection, will help you to manage the ways your mind and body influence each other. Being aware of your thoughts for even just a few minutes each day is a start.

Checking in with yourself as often as possible and monitoring your thoughts will serve you well. When you manage your thinking to that which is more positive, or you allow your body to experience positive things such as exercise, relaxation and good health, the mind-body connection improve tenfold.

MEASURING ENERGY FLOW USING THE SUD SCALE

EFT uses a scoring system to measure the depth and intensity of a problem and this scale is called SUD (Subjective Unit of Distress) it measures on a scale of 0 - 10.

0 equates to feeling neutral and 10 equates to feeling high emotional distress. It's helpful as you work through various problems to measure before and after tapping, the level of distress you begin and end with.

This scale was introduced in 1969 by Joseph Wolpe.

Using this scale helps you to identify how much the problem may be affecting your physical and emotional wellbeing.

SUD Scale　　Subjective Unit of Distress										
0	1	2	3	4	5	6	7	8	9	10
Neutral Emotional Charge		Intensity of emotion builds				Intense emotions escalate			Maximum emotional charge	
Low intensity of emotions		Emotions often manageable but not ideal				Emotions often overwhelming			High intensity of emotions	

RESOLVE AND DISSOLVE YOUR PROBLEMS USING EFT

By making a commitment to yourself to apply EFT to work through the things that may have been holding you back in life and love, you really step into your own power in resolving and dissolving past hurts and fears.

Choosing to take personal responsibility right here and now to commit to yourself and taking responsibility for the changes that you would like in your life, is one of the best investments you will ever make. It's through regularly working on yourself that the biggest changes occur.

EFT can be applied to any area of your life and used to transform the complete range of all emotions EFT has the capacity to change your life for the better, clearing the past and creating a space for the new.

I advise using EFT as soon as possible, in your everyday life. Whenever and how frequently you use EFT is a personal choice. You can never tap too much, only too little.

EFT has a positive chain reaction and works not just on one main issue but all the little connecting issues that are related to a problem. If you have any doubt at all about whether or not to tap on problem, tap and see what what changes as a result.

As you read through Find YOU, Find LOVE you will become aware of your old patterns, outdated behavioural responses and how you may have been unintentionally getting in your own way or blocking your own success, sabotaging love relationships without being aware of what you were doing.

We all do it at some point in our lives, unwittingly sabotage ourselves, as the fear of the unknown is greater than the fear of what is. That is all about to change.....

EFT Tapping Points

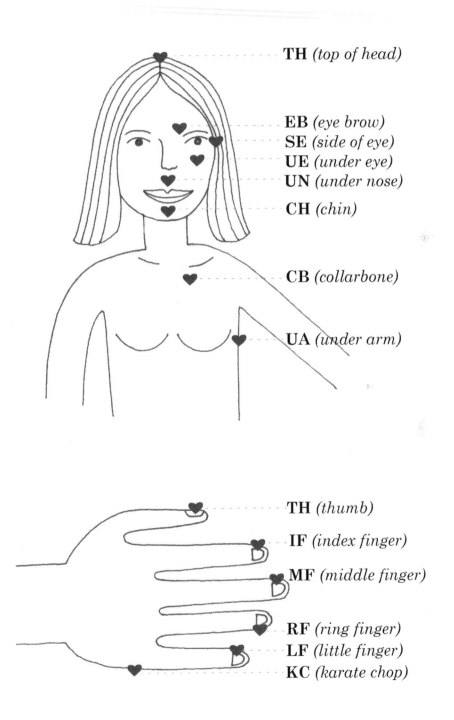

TH *(top of head)*

EB *(eye brow)*
SE *(side of eye)*
UE *(under eye)*
UN *(under nose)*

CH *(chin)*

CB *(collarbone)*

UA *(under arm)*

TH *(thumb)*

IF *(index finger)*

MF *(middle finger)*

RF *(ring finger)*
LF *(little finger)*
KC *(karate chop)*

THE EFT PROCESS:

TAP IN THIS ORDER

- karate chop point KC
- Top of the head TH
- Eyebrow EB
- Side of the eye SE
- Under the eye UE
- Under the nose UN
- Under lower lip CH
- Collar bone CB
- Under the arm UA
- Thumb TH
- Index finger IF
- Middle finger MF
- Ring finger RF
- Little finger LF

STEP 1 Recall a specific past or current problem/event that you wish to work through. Be as clear as possible what the feeling, issue or problem is that you want to work on. Is the problem thought based, behaviour based, physical or emotional?

STEP 2 Determine the level of distress you feel on a scale of one to ten (0 not being a problem and 10 being intense). You may wish to write this down, so that you can compare the before and after scores so that you can measure the reduction in distress going down in between each tapping round.

Gather the various aspects of the problem. Where in your body do you feel the emotional issue most strongly? Does it have a colour, a shape? What does it feel like? What is its weight? Does it have a smell, a sound, a taste? We store information through our senses – visual (seeing), auditory (hearing), kinaesthetic (feeling), gustatory (taste), olfactory (smell) and the way we store a memory/emotion often relates to one or more dominant sense.

STEP 3 "SET UP": The set up is where we begin the actual EFT tapping process. While tapping with our finger tips on the karate chop point, on the side of either hand in line with the little finger, we use a 'set up statement' repeating it three times.

The traditional EFT set up statements is, "Even though I have this (name the problem or issue here), I deeply and completely love and accept myself." Repeat this statement or variations of this statement on this point three times before moving on to the additional sequential tapping points. If this statement is uncomfortable for you, you may prefer to select an alternative set up statement from the choices offered further on or, make one up of your own that feels comfortable for you.

STEP 4 Follow the full tapping sequence after you have started with the karate chop point. You can tap on either side of your body with either hand. Tap round all the tapping points lightly with the finger pads in sequence, about five to seven times on each point, while repeating the reminder phrase (this is a shorter version of the problem) i.e. the issue, symptom you are working on (this stress, this anger, this disappointment, this lack of self belief)

STEP 5 Repeat several rounds of tapping in this manner until you feel the problem starting to reduce in emotional intensity

STEP 6 Reassess the emotional intensity of the problem using the scale 0-10

STEP 7 Continue tapping round all points with further rounds, until the emotional intensity reduces to a 0

STEP 8 Now, think about the original problem and see if any emotional intensity remains

STEP 9 If any part of the problem that you started with remains, work through the various aspects of the problem and persist with tapping through the tapping sequence, until the problem subsides. " Even though I have some remaining (state the problem), I deeply and completely love and accept myself". Sometimes when we're tapping on a problem, it can change. It may feel as if the energy of the problem has shifted and moved around the body, some aspects of the problem, including the emotions that surface may have changed too. If necessary, to re-evaluate the problem and the aspects of it, start the procedure again from Step 1 and work through the aspects of the problem that have come up or changed as a result of tapping.

EFT SET UP STATEMENTS

There is a choice of EFT set up statements that you can use to transform your emotions. Decide from the following statements which statement feels right for you. Each set up statement is repeated three times, either using the same statement or a variation of the problem before moving on with the additional sequential tapping points.

You will repeat the ending statement while tapping on the karate chop point on the side of the hand in line with the little finger i.e.:

''Even though I have this (name the problem or issue here), I deeply and completely love and accept myself''

"Even though I have this fear that I will get hurt again in relationships, I accept who I am and how I feel".

"Even though I have this fear that my relationships won't work out I allow myself to move through this".

ALTERNATIVE EFT SET UP STATEMENTS

If the traditional EFT set up statement feels uncomfortable in any way i.e. ''I deeply and completely love and accept myself'' select an alternative below which you resonate with more.

- I'm learning to love and accept myself
- I am willing to love and accept myself anyway
- I accept myself just the way I am
- I accept who I am and how I feel
- I am special, unique and valuable
- I choose to bo ok with this
- I'm open to accepting myself just the way I am
- I've decided to be more open and accepting of how I feel
- I allow myself to move through this
- I'm in the process of loving and accepting myself
- I honour myself
- I am learning to love, accept and appreciate all parts of me
- I'm a good person
- I accept all of me and the feelings I have
- I accept that I'm doing the best that I can
- I am beginning to feel it's ok for me to let this go
- I allow myself to move through this
- I've decided to take it one day at a time
- I choose to find new ways to work this out

Be persistent. EFT is convenient, quick and easy to use. It can be used as a standalone form of support for a short period of time, to work through one specific issue or, on a regular basis, to work through a range of problems. EFT will help to reduce the emotional intensity of many issues, past, present and future.

You have to love yourself because no amount of love from others is sufficient to fill the yearning that your soul requires from you - Dodinsky

TAKING STOCK

 **Practical Exercise
(15 minutes)**

Answer the following questions and record your answers in your journal. If as you work through the questions you feel any uncomfortable emotions coming up, apply EFT. This will support you in dissolving and resolving the emotional overwhelm you may have been carrying, related to different areas of your life and life experiences.

Be patient with yourself, and know that as long as you are tapping and using EFT to shift and change the energy around the things that have been holding you back, progress can be made.

- **What negative thoughts, feelings and emotions about love and relationships do you suffer from the most?**
- **Who or what triggers these thoughts, feelings and emotions the most?** (this could be a person, situation or a place)
- **List in brief, the top ten most traumatic events that you have experienced related to love and relationships**
- **Who or what is holding you back from having a loving and a positive relationship?**
- **What is preventing you from being more loving towards yourself?**
- **Who from your past are you carrying any anger or resentment towards?**
- **What limiting negative beliefs do you have about love?**
- **What limiting negative beliefs do you have about relationships?**
- **What limiting beliefs do you have about yourself?** (i.e. I'm not good enough)
- **What positive and empowering beliefs would you like to have about yourself, in love and relationships instead of the above?**

Your life begins to change the day you take responsibility for it – Steve Maraboli

TRANSFORM YOUR THOUGHTS AND FEELINGS USING EFT

**Practical Exercise
(10 minutes)**

I have included this word bank of possible thoughts, feelings and emotions that you may experience regularly. Read through the list and record the emotions that you experience the most and apply EFT to each until you feel the emotional intensity reducing. Acknowledging that we are experiencing the emotion is the first step towards transformation. We do not deny having any of our emotions. We welcome them in order to release them.

Alone	Angry	Annoyed
Anxious	Ashamed	Apprehensive
Bad	Betrayed	Blamed
Bored	Bullied	Burdened
Cheated	Confused	Controlled
Compared	Compulsive	Criticised
Damaged	Defeated	Dependent
Depressed	Devalued	Devastated
Disappointed	Disapproved of	Disconnected
Embarrassed	Emotional	Emotionless
Excluded	Exhausted	Exposed
Failure	Fearful	Flawed
Forgotten	Fragile	Frustrated
Grief	Guilt	Hate
Haunted	Heartbroken	Helpless
Hopeless	Horrified	Humiliated
Hurt	Imposed upon	Impatient
Inadequate	Incompetent	Incomplete
Insufficient	Insecure	Insignificant
Invalidated	Invisible	Jealous
Judged	Labelled	Lied to

Lonely	Lost	Manipulated
Misled	Mistreated	Misunderstood
Mixed up	Neglected	Nervous
Not good enough	Offended	Overwhelmed
Panicked	Paranoid	Passive
Petrified	Picked on	Powerless
Punished	Put Down	Quiet
Regret	Rejected	Resentment
Responsible	Scared	Selfish
Shamed	Small	Stressed
Stupid	Trapped	Unappreciated
Uncertain	Unhappy	Used
Unworthy	Victimised	Violated
Vulnerable	Worried	Worthless

REWRITING THE PAST

Use this section to identify self limiting beliefs, fears and doubts. Include past hurts and any unresolved emotions or attachments you may have to past relationships that you feel are holding you back. It's important to also consider how your emotions get triggered in or out of relationships.

It will be helpful to note what or who you react to - your triggers - and to explore your earliest memories of feeling the same way. This could be anything from not feeling listened to, being ignored, not being considered, or the perception that you are not loved or are an inconvenience in some way.

**Practical Exercise
(10 minutes)**

In your journal, copy out a blank version of this chart. Use the left hand column to record the negative beliefs that you wish to change and the right hand column to record your new and empowering beliefs, learning and wisdom gained after applying EFT.

Using EFT to clear past negative experiences will enable you to move towards achieving what you want from life, love and relationships. You can literally rewrite the past with a new set of empowering beliefs.

Not all emotions and beliefs are opposites, as you become free of the emotions and beliefs that have been limiting you, you will be able to create new ones.

Self Limiting Belief	New Belief
Doubts or fears from the past including unresolved emotions	Learning and applying wisdom and using the past to motivate you to resolving problems
1. I'm afraid I will never meet anyone	1. There is every reason to believe that I will meet someone
2. I'm afraid of getting hurt again	2. The past need not influence the future, I am wiser and have learnt from past experience
3. I'm disappointed that things didn't work out with ...	3. Just because things didn't work out with my ex doesn't mean things won't work out with my new partner
4. I'm saddened that ...	4. All emotions are energy and I know that my sadness will pass

**EFT Practical Exercise
(20 minutes +)**

Use the following practical exercise and apply EFT while tapping through and speaking out loud the statements if they are part of your experience. Use the statements below as a guideline of how to form your own tapping statements that relate to your own love and relationship challenges. Apply EFT until you feel the emotions connect to each statement subside

- **Even though I have experienced a parent not loving me in the way I needed, I deeply and completely love and accept myself**
- **Even though in my past I have been hurt by others, I let go of this negativity now**
- **Even though it feels unsafe to love again, I am willing to be open to giving and receiving love again**
- **Even though I don't love myself because of .... what if it doesn't matter anyway and I choose to love myself now**

- Even though I haven't always taken care of myself and treated myself with respect, I choose to love and respect myself now
- Even though people have said hurtful things, I choose to see myself in a positive light
- Even though name the person/people here hurt me and it's hard to forgive them, I'm choosing forgiveness to set myself free
- Even though I don't agree with what ......did, I forgive myself and I forgive them too
- Even though I'm scared of being hurt I know, that unless I am open to love, I am just hurting and limiting myself
- Even though I don't like the way I look, what if I'm lovable just the way I am?
- Even though I'm broken hearted, I choose to move on anyway
- Even though I have felt in the past that I'm not good enough, what if I'm ok just the way I am?
- Even though I feel insecure, I forgive and love myself right now

You are loved, just for being who you are, just for existing, you don't need to do anything to earn it, your shortcoming, your lack of self esteem, physical perfection or social and economic success, none of that matters, no one can take this love away from you and it will always be here – 'Be Love Now' Ram Dass

 Alternative ways to tap - 21 Day Field Clearing Technique (5-10 minutes + daily for 21 consecutive days)

You might like to use the EFT tapping script below for twenty one consecutive days or more and notice what changes for you. The 21 Day Field clearing Technique works well on longer standing issues.

This exercise has been adapted from Matrix Reimprinting using EFT by Karl Dawson and Sasha Allenby.

Karate chop: Even though I haven't always felt loved, I totally love and accept myself anyway (repeat three times)

Top of the head: I haven't always felt loved

Inner eyebrow: I want to always feel loved

Side of the eye: I choose to always be loved

Under the eye: I love to always be loved because...then list all the reasons why you want to be loved, either in your own mind or out loud

Under the nose: I am open to receiving love

Chin: As you tap, ask yourself what you would hear inside your own mind or from another person, if you were loving towards yourself, or they were loving towards you

Collar bone: As you tap, ask yourself what you would need to regularly do to be more loving towards yourself, or receive the love offered by others. Either speak the things out loud, or simply bring them to mind as you tap through the points

Under the arm: Ask yourself how you would feel if you regularly acted in a way that was more loving towards yourself. Get into that feeling of being more lovable and open to love. If you have difficulty in getting into this place of feeling, simply remember a time and place where you were kind and loving to yourself or, when another person showed kindness and love towards you

Thumb: As you tap, choose an image or symbol that you associate with love and take this image into your mind

Index finger: As you tap on your index finger with the image in your mind, think about and see, sense, or imagine all the neural pathways in your brain connecting with this image and make this picture and experience your reality

Middle finger: As you tap, send a signal to every cell in your body, that love is your new reality

Ring finger: As you tap on your ring finger, take the image or symbol of love into your heart, making the image bright and clear and really feel what it feels like to experience the energy of love flowing through you

Little finger: As you tap, send the image out from your heart (spend a couple of minutes doing this), and enjoy sending the love through you into the outside world

LEARNING TO LOVE YOURSELF IS THE GREATEST LOVE OF ALL

In the words of George Benson and later Whitney Houston, 'Learning to love yourself is the greatest love of all'.

Creating loving relationships comes from loving yourself first. Your outer world will mirror back to you your inner world. What you believe about yourself both the positive and the negative, you may attract back towards you. When you are more tender and loving towards yourself, you will have reflected back to you boundless opportunities for love.

You have an opportunity right now to learn from the past and to work towards treating yourself differently, learning to respect, love and honour yourself completely. It's time to start appreciating and acknowledging yourself for who and what you are. Any time you come away from your truth, your wholeness, your centre and lose sight of your greatness and your lovability, gently forgive yourself and go back to treating yourself with love, respect and care. When you slip back into old behaviours of self criticism, self judgement and harshness, think about what it was that made you act in an un-loving way towards yourself and be aware of any thoughts, words and actions that you expressed about yourself that were hard hearted and insensitive.

When you learn to be more loving and considerate to yourself first and foremost, your inner mirror reflects to the outside world that you are happy, content and already filled with love and this is what will show up for you...even more love!

EFT is such a wonderful resource as it can be used to work through the various emotions that surface when you feel unloved, rejected, unworthy etc

POSITIVE EFT

THE POSITIVE EFT PROCESS – YOU'RE GONNA LOVE THIS!

Silvia Hartman developed Positive EFT and the SUE Scale Subjective Unit of Experience) in 2009.

It is used to measure energy flow through the energy body from a minus ten to a plus ten. The scale scores where you shift from in terms of negative energy and what you shift to in terms of positive energy.

SUE Scale (Subjective Unit of Experience) Hartmann 2009

Use positive EFT when you feel you have cleared enough negative emotional charge around your love and relationship issues. It's best to clear first to reduce emotional intensity and then work up the positive scale to a +10

For Positive EFT it's best to stand up and to allow you body to also move around as you work through the process. It's a wonderful technique and energy can move quite quickly up and through your body. You may feel with this technique like laughing, giggling, smiling and moving about. My first experience of Positive EFT made me feel like running as the energy shift was so huge.

POSITIVE EFT – THE PROCESS

- Really think about the positive energy, emotion, thought, and feeling you want more of and think about what having more of this positive energy would mean to you and how much you want it. Let's for example assume you want more love?

- Score yourself as to how much love you feel you already have using the SUE Scale so that you can measure progress if you are on a low plus or a minus we basically want to move you all the way up to a +10, why would you want anything less?

- Start by placing both hands over your heart area (or you may prefer the centre of the chest where you might point to yourself when you say 'I am' or 'me') It doesn't matter which hand is on the top (your heart is on the left hand side of your body-you'd be surprised how many people get this wrong)

- Take in three deep breaths in and out stating the positive that you would like '' I want more love'' and say it like you mean it, allow your voice and tone to increase, say it with conviction and pride ''I WANT MORE LOVE''

- Tap lightly on each meridian point with your index and or middle finger making light contact with the area you are tapping on. Take a deep breath in and out at each point before moving to the next.

- Repeat your chosen positive word 'love' at each point. It is best to work on one positive at a time and not several choices at the same time and work towards getting a +10 for all choices.

- Keep calm and relaxed throughout and move your body if it feels like moving as the positive energy starts flowing.

- Take a moment at the end of each round of tapping with both hands back to the heart position and reflect on what you are feeling, where you are feeling the positive energy of love and what you have learned.

- At the end of each round of tapping you might like to reflect on how far up the positive love scale you have finished.

- Keep going tapping in a new round, repeating your positive word. Allow yourself to really want more love or whatever statement you have chosen. The aim is always to get you to a +10. Why stop at anything less!

- If you have an important date or something in the future connected with your relationships, love or anything else for that matter you might like to use the words "sending myself more love", or "sending love to the future me", or "sending more love to my future self" or "sending 'your name here' more love". This helps by giving you more of the positive energy that you want in the future.

It's best to always clear negative emotions before using positive EFT for maximum benefit. You may wish to use some of the word choices on the next page for general tapping in of positives

Love wins back what was never lost – Byron Katie

TURNING THE NEGATIVE TO POSITIVE

When we are able to operate and think from the place of 'what else is possible' so many things become possible.

Change work and tapping in the positives after clearing the negatives works beautifully together.

**Practical Power Exercise
(12 + minutes)**

You might like to work through a series of memories and emotions and turn those experiences to positives. This can be achieved by following the order below:

1. **Identify your subconscious fear/s about love and relationships (this equates to a belief) i.e. I'm not worthy of love**

2. **Measure how strong your fear is for each emotion on a scale of 1-10, ten being the most intense measure (SUDS/Subjective Unit of Distress)**

3. **Re-phrase the subconscious fear (Even though I have this fear of not being worthy of love I deeply and completely love and accept myself)**

4. Tap round the meridian points until the fear starts to move down the SUD scale to a 0

5. Once you have a achieved a neutral, zero score and converted the subconscious fear to a positive statement i.e. I am worthy of love, I am confident that I am lovable, I attract loving relationships to me

6. Keep tapping round the positive statement that you choose 'I want more love' until you go up the positive scale from a 0 up to a +10

7. As you work through resolving any negative emotions as long as the negative emotion is reduced down to a 0 (neutral) you can tap in any number of positives, working this way is wonderful and you may notice huge energy shifts as you literally transform your beliefs

8. An alternative option for this would be to chose a word from the positive 's below and follow the positive EFT process

I choose for myself to be:

Worthy	Lovable	Trusting
Hopeful	Complete	Loving
Content	Joyful	Giving
Affectionate	Caring	Open
Fulfilled	Strong	Curious
Satisfied	Peaceful	Vibrant
Excited	Whole	Cheerful
Light-hearted	Happy	Sparkling
Calm	Gratified	Centred
Serene	Compassionate	Kind
Empathic	Warm-hearted	Appreciative
Considerate	Thoughtful	Friendly
Confident	Receptive	Interested
Attractive	Passionate	Warm
Thankful	Inquisitive	Optimistic
Courageous	Playful	At ease
Comfortable	Encouraged	Relaxed
Reassured	Inspired	Determined
Brave	Dynamic	Loved
Unique	Sure	Comforted

Accepting	Assured	Content
Independent	Easy-Going	Enchanted
Enthusiastic	Kind Hearted	Open
Honest	Self Assured	Tender
Alive	Safe	Proud
Glad	Amazed	Adored
Embraced	Desired	Romantic
Tender	Sentimental	Gentle
Positive	Admired	Accepted
Attractive	Gorgeous	Harmonious
Successful	Valued	Welcoming
Lovely	Funny	Encouraging
Hugged	Graceful	Awesome
Adventurous	Creative	Engaging
Focused	Satisfied	Fulfilled

No one saves us but ourselves. No one can and no one may. We ourselves must walk the path – Buddha

After clearing and reducing any negative emotional charge around love and relationships using EFT, use Positive EFT to amplify the love already within you. Using positive EFT lifts and raises our energy vibration to that which is positive and loving.

When you are more loving and accepting of yourself, happy and content with who you are, you show up differently in the world. Others are able to sense how you feel about yourself and if you are thinking and feeling in loving ways and then you are more likely to attract love and loving relationships.

 Heart Based Exercise
(15 minutes)

As well as applying Positive EFT, complete the following love statements below either speaking them out loud, silently inside your own mind or using your journal. Re-read and tap through these statements every day adding additional statements of your own:

- **I love knowing that I deserve....**
- **I love being....**
- **I love feeling...**
- **I love allowing....**
- **I love choosing...**
- **I love enjoying...**
- **I love exploring...**
- **I love that I have decided to...**
- **I love knowing that...**

Once you have completed these statements adding your own endings tap around your points (speaking them out loud or inside your own head)

If any old or negative emotions do come up, go back and clear them using the traditional EFT method and then come back to Positive EFT.

When was the last time you said 'I love you' to yourself?   If it was a long time ago or never, now is the perfect time to change that.

You now have all the tools that you need to be more loving towards yourself. When you can express love to yourself easily, the gift of love comes back to you. EFT is a process and as you work though old hurts, fears, setbacks and disappointments, this will move you into a space of being freer emotionally to explore what you want for your future and taking you into the space of being open to more love. Without the burden of past negative emotions weighing you down and by making a commitment to yourself to apply The Spotlight Process and EFT to your life, you are literally closing one door and opening another.

When you are able to love and accept yourself totally for who you are, life unfolds and supports you in a way that you may never have dreamed possible. You are completely self sufficient, whole, resourceful and complete without the love of another.

Once you have got into that space of believing 100% that you are lovable, exactly as you are, there is an increased chance that a new love will turn up, or existing relationships will improve, as you stay centred in your wholeness and ability to love yourself, regardless of external events or people.

Many people notice improvements and positive changes after just a few EFT sessions. Others, depending on life experience, may prefer to work a little longer through those issues which have become old outdated stories stopping them from living the life they truly deserve. The good news is, the more you apply EFT, the better your life gets. You are no longer reacting; you simply go with the flow of life, taking it in your stride, knowing that your love bucket will be ever full!

First comes the thought, then organisation of that thought, into ideas and plans, then the transformation of those plans into reality. The beginning as you will observe, is in your imagination – Napoleon Hill

Chapter 2

The Spotlight Process

The Spotlight Process

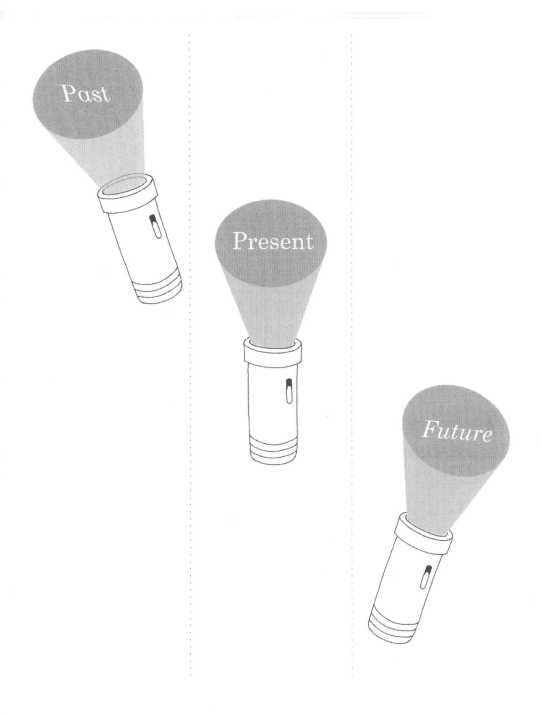

THE SPOTLIGHT PROCESS - BRINGING BALANCE TO YOUR THINKING

Having worked therapeutically with many people over the years, I have seen how people were limiting themselves and their love and relationship goals because of their negative thinking.

They were either spending too much time thinking about the past, focusing entirely on current problems, or projecting catastrophic and disabling fears into the future.

I developed The Spotlight Process to help you acknowledge where you have been spending most of your thought time and will guide you to work out where your thoughts may be out of balance and how to change them.

 Insightful Questions

WHERE HAVE YOU BEEN SHINING YOUR SPOT LIGHT?

- **Are you stuck in the past thinking about all the things you regret not having done? Do you feel angry and bitter about your choices? Do you wish you have your life all over again wishing you knew back then what you know now?**

- **Do you spend a lot of time thinking about your current problems, feeling like there's no way out? Do you feel overwhelmed, bogged down, fed up and tired of life?**

- **Are you constantly evaluating, judging and filtering for all the things that could go wrong for you in the future? Are you scared of taking risks and things going wrong? Do you find it hard to trust, to live, to love?**

 **The Spotlight Process**

Now is the perfect time to apply The Spotlight Process to your own life simply by examining your thoughts.

- Wherever you are at this moment, I invite you to think about a spotlight and the light that shines from it. Whether you see it, sense it or imagine it, think about that spotlight right now. This ray of light could be a light in the form a torch, a lighthouse, a stage spotlight. Whatever spotlight comes to mind is perfect for you.

- Think of this ray of light as a ray of your thoughts, feelings and emotions. This light can shine back into your past, ahead to your future or into this very moment.

- This is your spotlight. You are in control of shining the light. You are the director of where you narrow your beam and what you choose to illuminate and think about. Whatever you shine your light on, you will experience.

- Using The Spotlight Process consider where you have been spending most of your thought time?

Past?

Present?

Future?

- Examine your thoughts & feelings about past are they positive or negative in terms of love and relationships?

- How do you feel about your current relationship status in the present?

- Consider what concerns and fears you have about the future of your relationships?

Using this process you will gain insights into what has been holding you back from finding you and finding love.

THE SPOTLIGHT PROCESS - KEY QUESTIONS:

I suggest you copy these questions into your journal to carry them around with you until the questions become part of your natural thought process.

1. Where is my thinking right now? (Past, Present or Future?)
2. What proportion of my thinking is negative?
3. How does it affect me when I focus on the negative?
4. Where is the evidence that what I think will happen will happen?
5. What do I want instead of thinking or feeling this way?
6. Coming from my heart instead of my head what would love do here?

- **Reflect on your learning's from using The Spotlight Process**

- **Where have your thoughts been most of the time?**

Past?

Present?

Future?

- **What do you want to move on from?**

- **Establish where you want to be in the future, what are your love and relationship goals?**

- **Consider the actions you will need to take to change your thinking**

- **What do you need to stop doing?**

- **What do you need to start doing?**

- **What do you need to do differently?**

When you are clear about where you have been spending your thought time and how this may be limiting you, the path ahead is brighter and more achievable, using this process will support you into brining your thoughts into balance and what you need to do to change them.

PAST – PRESENT – FUTURE – WHERE ARE YOU SHINING YOUR LIGHT?

• **Past:** If your light is always in the past, you cannot see the future.

• **Present:** If you're bogged down with current problems and that's all you're thinking about and focusing on, it's impossible to move on in the direction of your dreams and create the future you would like.

• **Future:** If you're worrying about the future and you don't take any action to achieve the things you'd like, you stay stuck where you are. When you shine your light in only one direction and thoughts are negative and limiting, it's impossible to see the light in other areas of your life.

USING THE SPOTLIGHT PROCESS ON THE STORIES IN YOUR MIND

From this moment on, when you get caught up in a story in your mind, please take a moment and reflect:

- **What part of your story is a replay of what happened in the past?**
- **How often do you tell this story?**
- **When you tell this story, how do you feel?**
- **Is your story one that you are creating about the future with a negative expectation based on the past?**
- **How is thinking in this way limiting you?**
- **What are the consequences of thinking this way?**
- **What do you want instead?**

When your story is a replay from the past or is a negative projection into the future your body responds as if you are actually experiencing fear simply because you are thinking about it. The memory isn't real though your mind and body may think it is real and project fear of attack into situations that are really quite safe. Our unconscious mind will do everything it can to keep us safe even if there is no actual risk. It's a self protection mechanism.

FLIGHT, FIGHT AND FREEZE RESPONSE – HOW YOUR BODY REMEMBERS TRAUMA

Many of you will have heard of the fight and flight response though not everyone is aware of the freeze response.

We are animalistic creatures and when we think there is a threat of danger (real or imagined) or bodies naturally go into fight, flight or freeze response. We store the information or what we believe to be true about the threat in our subconscious minds and unless we release the freeze response (using EFT helps with this) it's possible that we will keep being re-triggered every time a new situation/event seems to be a similar threat to our original experience of a threat to our survival.

It was helpful to operate from this awareness when we were cave man and woman as our life depended on it. We would either stay and fight or run from attack though if the fear is too great and if we weren't able to run or fight we would freeze instead (like a rabbit caught in the headlights of a car). While in 'freeze response' we might pass out, remove ourselves from our bodies (this is called disassociation) we may also experience having no sensation of pain or sometimes no memory of the event at all.

You may find yourself going into fight, flight and freeze response daily if you find yourself in a situation that triggers you. These responses release chemical and emotional reactions in the body which re traumatise the system all over again as if the original fear and threat to survival was happening all over again.

EFT helps to release the freeze response and reduces the flight or flight response which in turn helps us to transform emotions and the think differently about our beliefs around fear of attack and threat to survival.

If you would like to read more about the fight, flight and freeze response you might like to discover the works of Dr Robert Scaer author of The Body Bears the Burden: Trauma, Dissociation and disease which goes into more detail about these responses.

The Spotlight Process will help you to work out where your thinking may be stuck or limited and it will support you in moving on from negative beliefs about yourself, love and relationships, to those which are more positive and life changing.

EXPLORING THE NEGATIVE IMPACT OF YOUR PAST

Take some time out to answer in your journal the following Power Questions.

- **What negative thoughts, feelings and emotions about love and rela-tionships do you experience the most?**

- **Who or what triggers these thoughts, feelings and emotions the most?** (This could be a person, situation or a place) be aware of your senses here (what are you seeing, hearing, feeling, smelling or tasting that may be trig-gering you?)

- **What are the top ten most traumatic events that you have experienced related to love and relationships?**

- **Who or what is holding you back from having a loving relationship?**

- **What is preventing you from being more loving towards yourself?**

- **Who from your past are you carrying any unresolved emotions towards?** (i.e. resentment, anger)

Answering these questions will give you an insight into the unresolved emotions that you are still carrying around with you. Often when we carry round baggage from the past it weighs heavy on us, zapping our energy as well as our hopes and dreams.

Hope is being able to see that there is light despite all of the darkness – Desmond Tutu

JANICE - A CASE STUDY UTILISING THE SPOTLIGHT PROCESS AND EFT

Janice was a classic example of letting the past limit her up until the point we met. Janice sought my help to try and work out the mess in her mind, she was feeling overwhelmed and felt like there was no escape: a prisoner in her own mind and by her own doing. Janice had a constant gremlin babbling away inside her mind telling her she was foolish, useless and that she mustn't speak up or think well of herself in any way.

After working with Janice for a while, we uncovered some of her childhood memories growing up at home and school where she was told to keep quiet, to be seen and not heard and quite clearly not to think too much of herself as it was deemed selfish and egotistical. She was frowned upon by her parents and teachers if she showed any emotions such as anger, sadness or frustration. It felt unsafe for her to express herself for fear or reprimand or criticism, so she closed down. She acted like a 'good girl' at all times and went to bed sobbing most nights feeling desperately lonely, feeling unheard and unloved. Janice stopped showing what she felt (it was too risky for her to be real both at home and school). She felt insignificant, unloved and invisible for much of her life and this had carried on into adulthood until she came to work with me.

At the age of forty five, Janice was still listening to the internalised voice of her parents and teachers reprimanding her as a child, she constantly replayed the conditions that her parents and teachers had set for her as a child, right through into her adult life (this is the story in her mind that she was constantly replaying and reacting from until she uncovered where her story came from using The Spotlight Process)

There is no blame here, Janice's teachers and parents were communicating in a way that they learnt through their own upbringing and learning experiences, they were simply telling her exactly what their parents told them and their parents before them, to be seen but not heard. Janice was in conflict with who she intrinsically believed herself to be as an individual - and who she was told she could and could not be, based on what her parents and teachers told her.

Running with the belief that she was invisible, unloved and mustn't speak up, meant that Janice was incredibly shy. She had little self belief, put herself last in her family and constantly put other people's needs before her own. Janice didn't speak up when she felt she was being taken advantage of, she never gave her honest opinion in important matters, all of which lead to intense anger, desperation and a sense of overwhelm. Janice really did believe that love meant looking after other people and that love was conditional and that you could only be 'good enough to be loved' if you didn't show your emotions or give an opinion.

Janice had spent most of her life feeling powerless and inadequate; she was unhappy in her marriage and came to me in a state of grief and despair, not trusting that she was capable of making the right choices for herself or her family, doubting that she was able to make the simplest of decisions without seeking clarification and approval that it was ok to do so.

Janice had spent much of her life reacting from her childhood beliefs that she formed about herself in school and through parental conditioning. She formed many limiting beliefs about how she thought she should be rather than who she was and she continued to respond from the little girl inside her rather than responding from her adult self, until she became aware during our work together that this way of responding was self limiting.

The beliefs that Janice formed in childhood were she realised were no longer the best way of running her life and that having her teachers approval was no longer necessary not that she was a fully grown woman. She discovered that as an adult it was ok for her to set personal boundaries with her parents and speak up about the things that were important to her and her own family.

As soon as you become aware of your own limiting beliefs and where the voice of judgement and reprimand comes from, you can gain a sense of awareness that the old, outdated, perceptions and judgements can have a detrimental impact on you.

You can change your beliefs and work through any personal limitations using The Spotlight Process and EFT, enabling you to let go of the past and move on with new found certainly towards finding out who you really are.

When you become more of who you are and less of who you are not, self love and acceptance become easier and opens up a world of loving opportunity all around you.

Practical Exercise using The Spotlight Process (15 minutes)

Periodically throughout the day and at the end of each day, use The Spotlight Process to take stock of where you have spent most of your thought time (past, present or future) and answer the following questions which complement the process beautifully.

- **What have I been focusing on?**
- **Where have my thoughts been (past, present or future?)**
- **How have I been talking to myself for the last hour or two?**
- **Have I been talking to myself in a kindly way or a critical way?**
- **What images, stories, thoughts or feelings have experienced today that have caused me distress?**
- **Which emotions and feelings have I experienced the most today?**
- **Have I been thinking about the future negatively or positively?**
- **What advice can I give myself so that tomorrow is a better day?**
- **What choices can I make that will take me closer to my love and relationship goals?**

You don't have to stay trapped in your thoughts just because you think them – Doug Dillon

USING YOUR PAST TO WORK FOR YOU

When you use the past to work for you rather than against you, instead of responding from the part of you (the child within) conditioned by your parents or caregivers you are able to reply from the adult you.

Responding from your adult self will support you to grow, to take action and to achieve great things you desire. Responding from the adult you, encourages you to take risks, to blossom, to treat yourself with love and kindness, to be the best that you can be and this is exactly what Janice did.

Janice made great progress in our time together using The Spotlight Process and EFT to work through her unresolved emotions from her past. She released years of built up anger and frustration that she had been carrying since her school days. She transformed the belief that she was unloved by her parents and released the sense of being powerless and inadequate to a sense of being in control of her life and her future.

Janice is now taking action. She speaks up clearly without feeling the need to explain her opinion; she is making time for herself and prioritising her own needs. Janice is also learning to love herself and to give herself the time, love and care that she didn't feel she had growing up and she is blossoming into a confident woman with a happy future ahead of her.

Insightful Questions

- **Do you identify with Janice in any way?**
- **How are you like her?**
- **What beliefs may have been passed down to you by your parents or caregivers etc that stop you being the real you?**
- **What beliefs have you formed about love and relationships based on your experiences?**
- **What did you believe in childhood that may no longer be true for you?**
- **How have you been using your past up to now, how has it limited you?**
- **Have you been using your past to work for you or against you?**
- **What has been the price you have paid or are paying now based on fear of the past repeating itself?**
- **What are you willing to change?**

The difficulties you meet will resolve themselves as you advance. Proceed and light will dawn and shine with increasing clearness on your path – Jim Rohn

Past – Present – Future

It's time to think about where you have been targeting your light. It's time to examine what has shown up, time to explore what needs to be cleared and resolved using EFT and from that point once you have cleared the past, your light will offer a ray of hope, bringing clarity and brightness to your future, sparkle and dazzle to your every day and most of all a warm glow of love from deep within the heart of you.

If you have been directing your light beam towards the pain and disappointments from the past, this is what you will see.

If you have been shining your light on failed relationships and lack of love, this is what you may attract in the future.

If you have been pointing the light on being alone, feeling lonely and on loneliness this only magnifies the feelings associated with being alone.

Whatever you shine the light on, it multiplies and grows, so shine it wisely. It's time to conserve energy and really stop and think about how your energy and light may be drained when you focus on lack rather than on possibility.

When you are ready to direct your beam to a positive future, your focus will bring to mind all that is possible, all that is achievable and all that is attainable. Your sunbeam of light will bring hope, create joy and illuminate potential, getting to the heart of love and relationships in far easier ways than you even imagined. You will have everything you need inside the pages of this book to guide you through to get to the heart of love and relationships.

AUTOMATIC NEGATIVE THOUGHTS AND HOW THEY LIMIT YOU

I invite you to listen....

Really listen....

Listen really carefully to what I am about to share with you....

This is a very important message....

There is no evidence at all except the story in your mind, that the negative aspects of your past will repeat themselves. It's a story that you may have been playing for way too long and when you play that story over and over your body hears that story and will respond with the fear, sadness, despair and the limitations that you place on your future. The future is not limited, but your thinking may be. It's time to change the story.

**Practical Exercise
(15 minutes)**

Read through and record how many of the automatic negative thoughts you identify with. You could simply tick them off if you are working through the physical book or if you are using a download version of the book, record in your journal which statements you think the most often. In doing so you will become aware of how many of your thoughts are automatic negative thoughts and made up stories that hold you back from having the love and relationships that you desire.

Automatic Negative Thought	Meaning
Mind reading	Assume that you know what people are thinking
Fortune telling	Predicting the future in a negative way
Judging	View yourself/others/events in terms of good/bad
Labelling	Giving global negative meanings about yourself and others
Ignoring the positives	Positive things aren't recognised or seem trivial
Blowing things out of scale	Believe that what will happen will be unbearable
Personalising	Assume self blame for negative events
Over generalising	See a global pattern of negatives based on a single event
'Should's'	Seeing people and events as to how you think they 'should' be
Negative filtering	Focus on the negative, ignoring the positive
Focusing on regrets	Focus on the idea that you should have done better in the past
Emotional reasoning	Allowing your feelings to guide your perception of reality
'What if' thinking	Thinking about all the things that could go wrong
All or nothing thinking	Black and white thinking/only good or bad - no in between
Blaming	Focusing on others as a source of your negative feelings
Unfair comparisons	Focus on others who you perceive are doing better than you
Inability to disconfirm	Reject any evidence that might contradict your negative thoughts

It's time to change your thinking. No one 'thinks you' that is the one thing that you do have control over. This two step process of identifying your thoughts and how you can change them works beautifully together.

**Power Questions and Practical exercise
(5-10 minutes throughout the day or at the
beginning and end of each day)**

Use the following twelve steps to bring your thoughts back into balance every time you recognise yourself going into automatic negative thinking about love and relationships. Copy out these statements and carry with you until the questioning becomes part of your natural thought process to bring yourself back each time you go into a story.

1 Am I confusing thought with fact?
2 Am I predicting the future negatively?
3 Am I jumping to conclusions?
4 Am I assuming I can do nothing to change my situation?
5 Am I overestimating the chance of disaster?
6 Am I thinking in all or nothing terms?
7 Am I only paying attention to the negative side of things?
8 Am I telling myself I'm not lovable because of things that have happened in my past?
9 Am I focusing on my weaknesses and forgetting my strengths?
10 What are the advantages and disadvantages of thinking this way?
11 Do my negative thoughts help or hinder me?
12 If I bring balance to my thinking, what would love do here?

Using The Spotlight Process, I will guide you to understand why you have been thinking the way you have been, enabling you to have a better understanding of how thinking in that old way of yours may have been limiting you.

Our thoughts can create many negative experiences, or many positive experiences; it's all down to the meaning and the beliefs and perceptions we place on things.

If the light is within your heart, you will find your way home – Rumi

Shining the light on your past

In this section, you will be creating a life inventory based on your past experiences to date and the most significant relationships at their highest and lowest points.

By completing this exercise, you may gain an awareness of how your relationship experiences have affected you negatively and also form an overview about the positive experiences of love and relationships that you can build upon.

Within the inventory which is a time line of your love and relationship events, please also record your emotions, thoughts, feelings and beliefs that were present at the time of the experience.

Think about a specific memory of an event and record the feelings and emotions that remain connected to that event itself and/or to the people in it i.e. anger, hate, fear, grief.

You may wish to explore the limiting beliefs section before completing the next exercise and look at the 'emotions word bank' in the EFT section, if you need to clarify what emotions you have experienced related to any limiting beliefs.

The Life Inventory can be used many times over across a range of personal experiences that you might wish to work through.

THE LIFE INVENTORY

The life inventory exercise can be used time and time again to work through any unresolved emotions from the past.

If you find the following Life Inventory exercise a little painful to work through, apply EFT as you go along in the knowledge that any journey of transformation begins by taking those first few steps and getting over the first few hurdles. If you prefer to work through this with guidance please do make contact via my website.

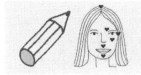

**Practical Exercise
(10-15 minutes)**

Spend just 10-15 minutes working through the inventory, listening intuitively to whatever answers present to you as you read through. Use the life inventory for each memory that you wish to transform.

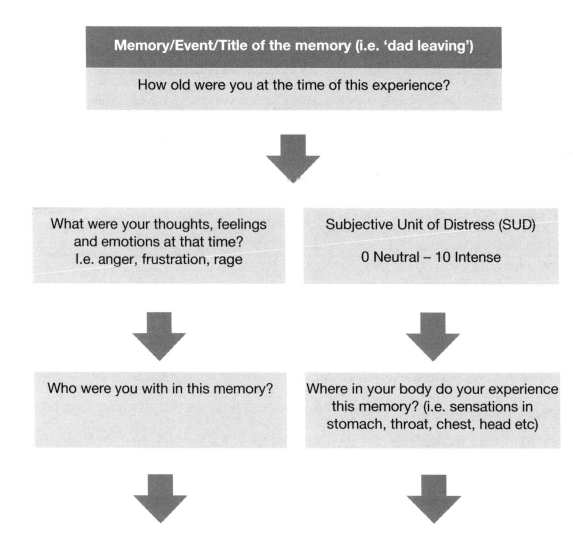

Memory/Event/Title of the memory (i.e. 'dad leaving')

How old were you at the time of this experience?

What were your thoughts, feelings and emotions at that time?
I.e. anger, frustration, rage

Subjective Unit of Distress (SUD)

0 Neutral – 10 Intense

Who were you with in this memory?

Where in your body do your experience this memory? (i.e. sensations in stomach, throat, chest, head etc)

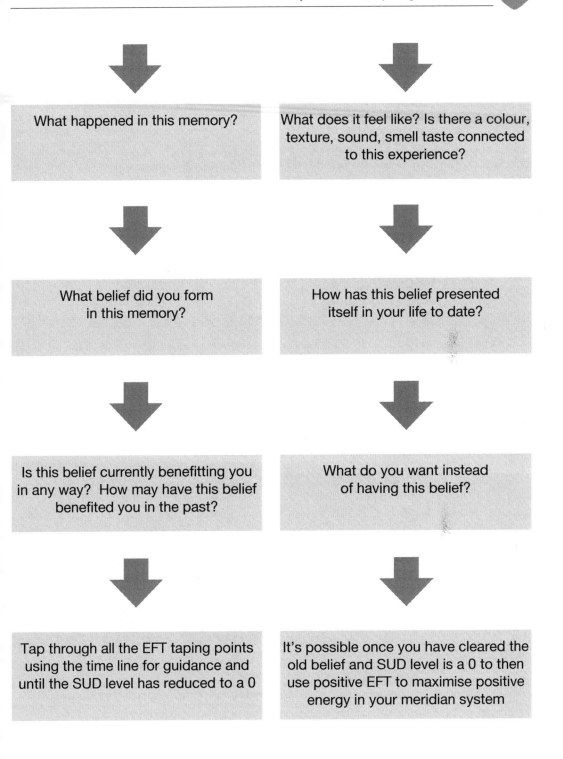

What happened in this memory?

What does it feel like? Is there a colour, texture, sound, smell taste connected to this experience?

What belief did you form in this memory?

How has this belief presented itself in your life to date?

Is this belief currently benefitting you in any way? How may have this belief benefited you in the past?

What do you want instead of having this belief?

Tap through all the EFT taping points using the time line for guidance and until the SUD level has reduced to a 0

It's possible once you have cleared the old belief and SUD level is a 0 to then use positive EFT to maximise positive energy in your meridian system

You will be working through emotions and limiting beliefs, applying EFT to the specific tensions within your relationships whether that be with family members, significant others, or friendship relationships.

This process is very cathartic, as it allows you to release the emotions that may have been holding you back from having successful relationships.

EFT stimulates and improves energy flow and releases the blocks that have become stagnant in the energy meridian system. Regular EFT tapping is encouraged to keep one's energy system in balance.

**Practical Exercise
(10-15 minutes)**

Record all the negative messages you heard from others, the phrases you heard, traumas large or small, any negative experience that still has an emotional impact on you that were experienced within those relationships.

Giving a voice to such unexpressed emotions and feelings helps us to bring resolution to the events that may have been painful to experience at the time.

There are several different ways to complete this exercise. You may wish to use the flow chart shown here or alternatively the grid below or sheets of flip chart paper, A4 loose sheets of paper, or on several different pages in your journal or a notebook.

The Time Line Grid (An alternative to the life inventory) is also a practical exercise which is slightly quicker to work though if you are short on time. (I have included some examples here for guidance)

Age	Event/Title of event/memory	SUD Level 1-10	Emotions	Beliefs formed
Age 5	First day at school	7	Fear	No one will like me
Age 7	Audition for play	8	Anxiety	I'm not good enough
Age 9	Granddad died	9	Grief	Everyone I love leaves me
Age 12	My body is changing	8	Shock	I need to hide my body

Age 14	My first boyfriend dumped me	9	Sad	It's not safe to love

- Record and organise into an order - from your first relationships with parents or caregivers and build up a time line to your most recent and current relationships. The relationships we have in childhood represent a huge proportion of our overall life experience and using the processes in this book will support you in breaking old cycles of behaviour.

- You will be recording all the key relationships in your life from the past and present. Include people no longer in your life, in terms of relationships ending or, the person with whom you had a relationship may be deceased. Relationships mean all family and extended family relationships; significant other relationships and all other relationships that you feel may be relevant such as friendships, first loves, etc.

- Include relationships at school with teachers and peers, relationships with religious institutions and relationships with working colleagues.

ALL RELATIONSHIPS, NEGATIVE AND POSITIVE, HAVE AN IMPACT ON US.

Following these processes, you will create a time line of the negative influences that may contribute to the lack of love you feel right now and how you are and have been experiencing relationships. You may recognise similar patterns repeating themselves across the history of your relationships and notice common feelings, thoughts, emotions and beliefs that are a theme throughout your inventory and time line.

By unearthing and digging up those old negative memories which have been growing like weeds and clogging up your thinking as well as your energy system, you will be able to operate from a new perspective where you know that the past is over and you are now in total control of your thoughts, feelings and emotions. You will have the tools and techniques at your fingertips to help you work through any memories that come up while you work through the exercises contained within.

A person can only give as much love as they have found within themselves - Daniel Chidiac

THE PAST IS OVER

The past is over. It's gone. It's history. Only your thoughts and energy of these negative experiences keep the past alive. It's only your thinking and the energy connected to this experience that remains, not the actual experience itself.

Record in your journal the answers to the power questions. You can turn your answers into the goals that you wish to achieve for the future connected with love and relationships.

**Power Questions
(15 minutes)**

- **What would it be like for you to move on from the past?**
- **How would your life change?**
- **What opportunities might come your way?**
- **What about love?**
- **What about relationships?**
- **How might your relationships be different if you choose right now to put the past behind you?**

You have the power to change your thoughts and your relationships. You are the driving force with the power to use your past to work for you and not against you. It's time to take a breath, time to stand still, time to spill out your monkey mind and discard the thoughts which no longer serve you and only put back in the thoughts that make you feel good. You are going to re-discover love with the absence of fear.

IT'S TIME TO STOP SHINING THE LIGHT ON THE PAST BECAUSE THAT'S NOT WHERE THE FUTURE IS.

I'm with you, I have your hand, I am beside you all the way, trust me, I believe in you and by the time we finish this journey, the past will just be a distant memory and your future an opportunity to discover all that is possible.

Turn your face to the sun and the shadows fall behind you – Maori Proverb

HONESTY IS THE BEST POLICY -
HOW TO RECOGNISE WHAT ISN'T WORKING IN YOUR LIFE

RECAP EXERCISE

- Familiarise yourself with the EFT tapping

- Use The Spotlight Process to track your thoughts

- Create an inventory of your time line of those negative, fearful beliefs and emotions that limit you, especially connected to love and relationships

- Observe and question what you have come to believe about love and relationships and why

- Keep a diary or journal to record any painful feelings, the situations in which those feelings arise and the self talk that makes you feel unhappy, use EFT to resolve these feelings and emotions

- Once you notice a thread of thought, examine whether the thoughts are propelling you forward towards joy and happiness, or whether your thoughts are holding you back from love?

- Identify ten of your own limiting beliefs about love and relationships, and then provide the evidence that make these beliefs real for you. These can then be resolved using The Spotlight Process and EFT

- Be aware from now on, when you are thinking or behaving in a way that may be limiting you. The words in our heads create thoughts, the thoughts create feelings , the feelings create/spur actions and actions create results (negative or positive)

- Let go of the beliefs that no longer serve you, using The Spotlight Process and EFT

The fact that someone else loves you doesn't rescue you from the project of loving yourself – Sahaj Kohli

Chapter 3

Beliefs

WHAT IS A LIMITING BELIEF?

A limiting belief is a mental block stored in your mind which limits your ability to achieve any goals you may set for yourself. A limiting belief acts as a barrier stopping you from achieving the success you desire and deserve, not only connected with love and relationships but in fact, with many other aspects of your life.

You will unconsciously organise your actions and behaviour depending on your beliefs, your beliefs are guiding principles and maps of how you make sense of the world. Some of your beliefs are not true and are simply thoughts that lead to your learnt behaviour and responses to people and events.

A limiting belief is a repetitive, habitual thought that you may think over and over and over again and it is my intention to guide you to discover what your negative beliefs and blocks to love and relationships might be.

Until you question your limiting beliefs, you may think that they are true and for this reason often your beliefs may come true, your limiting beliefs may act as self fulfilling prophecies even if the thought is undesirable.

Your limiting beliefs create your perception, through self talk and the internal dialogue that you run inside your head. You can talk yourself into doing or not doing something and what you believe influences your behaviour and performance.

You may find yourself staying in the safety of your comfort zone if a belief creates **F E A R** (**F**alse **E**vidence **A**ppearing **R**eal).

Look carefully and you will see that a limiting belief is nothing more than a thought that you believe to be true. The word 'be**LIE**f' itself includes the word LIE and until we explore our beliefs, perceptions and judgments, we will not be aware of what lies we have been telling ourselves about love and relationships that are no longer helpful to us.

As with judgements, limiting beliefs are nothing but patterns of thoughts. Just because your experiences in the past may have been true, it does not necessarily follow that they will continue to be true. You may find yourself building up walls of protection, trying to keep yourself safe from disappointment and heartache when in fact, it is these very walls that confine you and may stop you from having amazing relationships with yourself and others.

The conversations that you have inside your own mind may build on existing limiting beliefs, as you find yourself replaying the limiting beliefs over and over. Limiting beliefs can affect every part of your life, your work, your well being, your relationships and it is the beliefs we form about love in our early years, which impacts our lives in later years.

The limiting beliefs you have formed may be based on old fears, old hurts or old stories that have no relevance in the present moment. You may be blocked within certain areas of your life because of the beliefs that you are running, these beliefs do not just influence how positive or negative a relationship will be, our limiting beliefs impact all areas of our lives. Those beliefs will collapse the moment that you stop feeding the limiting belief and you can achieve this through the use of EFT and The Spotlight Process.

LIMITING BELIEFS AND LIFETIME ISSUES

In childhood we form many beliefs, in fact childhood represents a huge percentage of our overall life experience. The experiences we have growing up contribute to our inner dialogue and we may often tell ourselves that we are at fault in some way for whatever went wrong in our early years, even though this assumption was based on false information or a misguided perception.

Limiting core beliefs are the driving force in our lives and reflect our deepest vulnerabilities and pain and it's from the younger part of ourselves that we react from. Often our limiting core beliefs are what distance us from believing we are lovable and open to receiving love. Operating from the negative parts of ourselves, we cannot see the positives and opportunities available to us.

Working through these beliefs will bring more balance to your life and allow you the opportunity for personal transformation. This section supports you in gathering together the negative messages you heard about yourself or others growing up, the abuses, the traumas, and the conflicts. We have all had these kinds of experiences growing up and are affected in different ways. Giving a voice to our feelings and experiences, no matter how old we are now, gives us a new sense of liberation, a sense of empowerment and an opportunity to put the past in the past once and for all.

DISCOVERING LIMITING BELIEFS, BEHAVIOURS, THOUGHTS AND EMOTIONS

Here is a list of limiting beliefs that you may have formed about yourself, life and love relationships. Life issues related to core beliefs come from the perception of success, love, belonging, self worth, control, security, reality and reason. Core beliefs often grow stronger rather than weaker (as we are filtering for perceived evidence to back up the false belief).

**Practical Exercise
(10 minutes)**

Work through this list and record which limiting beliefs are true for you.

I'm unlovable	I can't do it	I'm flawed/imperfect
I'm unwanted	I'm different	I don't matter
I'm bad	I'm unforgivable	I must be approved of
Something bad will happen	Something must change for me to be ok	I'm powerless
The world is dangerous	I'm helpless	Life is hopeless
People take advantage	I must be perfect	I must be in control
I don't belong	I'm not good enough	I can't trust anyone
I'm a failure	I'm insignificant	I'm shameful
I'm a mistake	I'm helpless	I'm not special enough
I'm invisible	I'm guilty	I'm not interesting
I'm unworthy	I'm undeserving	I'm worthless
I'm incapable	I'm misunderstood	I'm abandoned
I will be betrayed	I'm unproductive	I'm unattractive
I'm Incompetent	I'm a failure	I'm a victim
I'm a burden	I'm dumb	I'm used
I'm alone	I'm bad	I'm guilty
I'm sinful	I'm confused	I'm trapped
I'm unlovable	I'm powerless	I'm inferior
I'm separated from God	I'm un-teachable	I'm vulnerable
I'm stupid	I'm weak	I can't get it right
I'm vulnerable	I'm unsuccessful	I'm ugly
I can't say no	I can't stand up for myself	I don't belong
I should not be here at all	I'm afraid	I'm fat
I'm unattractive	I'm left out	I don't deserve to be loved

GLOBAL ISSUES

Global issues relate to people who you may have had negative experiences with in your life and who have contributed negatively to your concept and beliefs about yourself.

Mother/Father	Religious Institutions/ Societal influence	Brothers/Sisters
Extended family/step family	Teachers/School/College	Other relationships

THE GOOD NEWS IS, BELIEFS AREN'T PERMANENT AND CAN BE CHANGED

Beliefs are nothing more than empowering or limiting thoughts. The beliefs we choose to give our attention to, guide our actions, behaviours and circumstances. Our core beliefs were developed at a time when we were children, when we had minimal ability to reason and think rationally for ourselves. The beliefs that were handed down to us were formed by our parents, mentors, teachers, environment and culture.

Core beliefs form the picture we paint of ourselves, a portrait of our own abilities, our worth, flaws, strengths and our relationships with others and with the world. Our beliefs establish the limits of what we think we can, or can't, achieve.

We behave in ways consistent with our beliefs and values. Our beliefs impact on much of what we do, the thoughts we think, our feelings and our physical symptoms. We delete, distort and generalise information by forming an intricate filter of opinions, emotions and memories and we only notice what we think supports the existing belief.

OUR THOUGHTS, ASSUMPTIONS AND BELIEFS INFLUENCE THE WAY THAT WE FEEL AND WHAT WE CHOOSE TO DO

A limiting belief is a thought, or series of thoughts, that stop us from moving forwards in life. Limiting beliefs could be based on past personal experiences or through witnessing the experiences of others. Limiting beliefs also shape the form of our thought patterns, including irrational thinking. We all, at some point, experience limiting beliefs. Until we examine what it is we believe and change any limiting beliefs to a more empowering belief, we are often stuck in the prison of our own thinking.

Beliefs have the potential to be changed by cultivating awareness; we can choose what it is we want to believe. Challenging a limiting belief with awareness, effective questioning and using The Spotlight Process and EFT, may seriously improve a person's sense of self worth, reduce fear, improve confidence, improve communication (internal and external dialogues) and open up all sorts of new and exciting possibilities.

WHAT ARE YOUR LIMITING BELIEFS?

Practical Exercise
(10 minutes)

MEASURING LIMITING BELIEFS USING
THE VOC SCALE (VALIDITY OF COGNITION)

To measure the how true a limiting belief may be for you there is a scale called The Validity of Cognition (VoC) Scale which is an individualised measure of beliefs, developed by Francine Shapiro.

Use the VoC Scale to check the percentage of your current self limiting beliefs rating them from a 0 when you have no belief at all and 100 when the belief feels completely true for you.

Read through the list below using the VoC Scale to identify which limiting beliefs are true for you.   Fill in the blanks where appropriate and add your own limiting beliefs that have been holding you back from love.

- **Fear of not being good enough**
- **Fear of not being loved**
- **Fear of rejection**
- **Fear of separation or loss of relationship**
- **Fear of failure**
- **Fear of being controlled by another**
- **Fear of success**
- **I don't deserve.....**
- **I am not worthy of.....**
- **I'm not lovable**
- **I'm too........**
- **I'm not.....**
- **I won't be able to.....**
- **It's impossible**
- **I can't.....**

- **Something bad will happen if.....**
- **What if it doesn't work out?**
- **What if I get hurt?**
- **What if my partner isn't faithful?**
- **What if I lose.....?**

You may be wondering right now how you can transform your limiting beliefs about love and relationships, so here goes:

Part of the process of changing limiting beliefs is cultivating awareness, so that we can distinguish the difference between:

- **What we'd like to believe**
- **What we think we should believe**
- **What we truly believe**

It is often our limited and negative thinking that holds us back from the things that we seek. Beliefs are often so unconscious that we seldom question them.

WITH EFFECTIVE SELF QUESTIONING, TAKING INTO ACCOUNT:

- **When the belief was formed**
- **Whose belief it is**
- **If that belief limits us or allows us to grow**
- **If the beliefs we hold are still appropriate for us**

Each of us has a choice and by choosing empowering beliefs about love and relationships, much can be changed in our lives for the better.

In order to change a limiting belief we need to change the internal picture and representation that we have of ourselves, of others and about the world around us, so that over time, our creative subconscious mind recognises new pictures and beliefs as a new reality and filters from a different perspective, instead of looking through dirty windows at the same dirt, we notice things we never saw before or experienced before.

If a limiting belief is based on a lie or is a belief formed by someone else's opinion, then it is time to change the belief. Challenging a limiting belief and working out where it comes from will provide enormous benefits.

Changing our beliefs offers a renewed sense of freedom and there is a willingness to take new risks once we decide to look at the world through new windows.

 Insightful Questions

Read through the following questions and notice your responses. You might be surprised at how unkind the thoughts you have about yourself really are.

- **How many of your thoughts about yourself are critical, blaming, bullying, shaming, ugly, unloving, downright rude and uncaring?**

- **What do you say to yourself on a regular basis that's damaging and unkind?**

- **How often do you project into the future the idea that love and relationships are pointless, that you're not good enough, slim enough, tall enough, worthy enough, attractive enough, smart enough?**

- **Would you talk to a best friend or a child the way you talk to and criticise yourself?**

- **Would you tell that person that they will never amount to anything, that they are useless, unlovable, worthless, stupid, ugly, shameful, inadequate, and pitying?**

Chances are, you would not say these things or others like them to another person and so it's time to stop speaking about yourself in a limiting way. It's time to stop the war against yourself, it's time to stop rejecting yourself, time to stop replaying the past, time to stop beating yourself up and playing small and time to get rid of the voice from the past.

It's time to start loving yourself and giving yourself the time, attention love and care that you deserve. It's time to listen to and meet your own needs by yourself for yourself.

The benefits of changing your limiting beliefs will be worth the commitment that you make to yourself. Your future is in your hands now and if you want to make the rest of your life the best of your life, EFT and The Spotlight Process will lead the way.

For longer standing emotions and limiting beliefs, patience and a willingness to use EFT regularly, will aid your progress towards overcoming more traumatic experiences.

Our main problems and limiting beliefs, come from the perception of our level of success, love, belonging, self worth, control, security, reality and reason. Getting really honest with yourself about the core beliefs that you may be running like a film or story in your mind, is a very important step in change work. Once we realise that a lot of the stories and movies that we play in our minds are outdated and unhelpful, we know what areas to work on transforming them through the use of EFT.

Practical Exercise – Brainstorm your beliefs (15-20 minutes)

Use this exercise to record of the limiting beliefs that you have formed about yourself, your life and love relationships. This exercise has been adapted from Transform Your Beliefs, Transform Your Life with the kind permission of Kate Marillat.

1. Use your journal or some pieces of paper to work through this exercise

2. From the list below, ask yourself how true each statement is for you. Measure using the VoC Scale the percentage that this belief is true for you out of 100% (100% being totally true for you and 0% being completely untrue)

3. Write down on separate pages in your journal or on pieces of paper each belief in the centre

4. List all the reactions, thought, feelings, memories and associations connected with this belief

5. Add any additional beliefs that you have that are limiting if they are not shown on the list provided

6. Use EFT to work through you limiting beliefs and connected emotions until the VoC Scale drops right down to 0

Be aware that some core beliefs come from our conditioning whilst growing up. There is no blame here on our caregivers, we were very young when we formed our core beliefs and at the time, these beliefs seemed to be appropriate for us. Core beliefs may be formed based on the following conditions:

- **Fear associated with rejection/not being lovable, worthy or approved of**

- **Fear associated with not meeting expectations, being good enough, adequate, recognised**

- **Fear associated with criticism, judgement, being made wrong, being told off, being compared**
- **Fear associated with people giving you attention, unwanted attention, smothering, feeling singled out, harassed, embarrassed**

Core beliefs can be likened to a table. At the top of the table is the limiting core belief. This is held up by the table legs which are formed from family conditioning, societal conditioning, emotional events, upset and trauma. Your core beliefs may also have many other beliefs underlying them supporting the core belief.

If you feel that you'd like to learn more about the science behind beliefs take a look at Transform Your Beliefs, Transform Your Life by Karl Dawson and Kate Marillat.

Remember, there is never any blame. Whatever you discover that shaped your beliefs (if you felt unloved, unimportant, ignored or rejected by a parent or significant other) it doesn't mean they didn't love you, it was purely the meaning and belief you placed on an event or series of events and experiences with the knowledge that you had at the time.

We forget as adults that many of the beliefs we formed in childhood are outdated, destructive and are often completely wrong. Working through and having an awareness of the memories that you would like transformed is the start to the road of finding you and finding love.

Joking aside, I would like to remind you of some old, outdated, beliefs that you may have moved on from already:

- Father Christmas
- The Tooth Fairy
- Monsters under the bed
- Fairy tales and other stories

As a child, you may have read (or had read to you) various fairy tales and stories. We know, as adults, that the likelihood of meeting a knight on a white charger in shining armour, or being kissed in our sleep by a handsome prince, might not be all that realistic. Though many women I have worked with, still hold onto the thought of having a fairytale relationship where there is only love, tenderness and togetherness, where life is blissful 100% of the time. Where there is never a cross word, tears or upset.

You can use EFT to explore and release any disappointments, sadness, regrets, hopes and dreams about the love and relationships that you have wished for and never experienced.

EFT need not be all serious and intense, it can be used with humour and it might even be interesting to explore the beliefs formed in childhood about these fairy tales and the princes and kings that we hoped to meet. We all have dreams and it's ok to have them, we just need to wake up from the fairy tale and reflect on what beliefs are appropriate for our lives right now.

 **Insightful Questions**

EFFECTIVE BE <u>LIE</u> FS QUESTIONING

Use the following open questions to uncover specifically your love and relationship beliefs. Record the answers in your journal as you go along.

- **What limiting negative beliefs do you have about love?**
- **What limiting negative beliefs do you have about relationships?**
- **What limiting beliefs do you have about yourself?**
  (i.e. I'm not good enough)
- **What love and relationship beliefs are influencing your life negatively right now?**
- **Where do these beliefs come from?**
- **How did you come to believe what you do?**
- **Are these beliefs your own or ones that were passed down to you?**
- **What does having those beliefs mean to you/say about you?**
- **What triggers these beliefs?**
- **What does this belief accomplish?**
- **Are the beliefs appropriate for you today, or ones that you picked up years ago and forgot to update?**
- **What are the beliefs you hold about yourself in terms of love and relationships?**
- **What is the negative impact of having these beliefs?**
- **Is there any benefit or reason for keeping these beliefs?**
- **What alternative beliefs could you choose?**

- **If you changed those beliefs, what would you be able to do that you can't do now?**
- **What happens when you change those limiting beliefs?**
- **What will you gain from letting go of these limiting beliefs?**
- **What positive and empowering beliefs would you like to have about yourself, love and relationships instead of the above?**

UNDERSTANDING BELIEFS AND PAST CONDITIONING

At this point in your life you may have many different beliefs about love and relationships running. When I say running, I mean running like movies running through your mind or running like taped conversations playing over in your head or an endless series of thoughts, feelings and emotions moving through you.

When you think of the love and relationship movies you have been playing in your mind can they be compared a romance with a happy ending or is yours more of a heartbreak hotel scenario?

These movies often represent a constant flow of negatives (the voice of our inner critic/voice of doom, like a parasite that eats away at us from the inside and a voice we start to believe in and feelings that we think are real). We replay over and over the same movies and the same story, until story becomes engrained. That movie or inner story then becomes a default behaviour that we respond to when presented with a situation that is like one we have experienced before and triggers off what we believe to be true. Most of what we react to has very little to do with a new experience and everything to do with past experiences (old movies)

Insightful Questions

Here are some general beliefs about love and relationships that you might be familiar with and may well form part of your own story or movie. Which statements do you identify with?

- **"Men/women are all the same"**
- **"Men/woman can't be trusted"**
- **"Men/women are selfish and only think about themselves"**

- **"Men/women will only let you down"**
- **"You're better off on your own"**
- **"Love hurts"**
- **"Nothing lasts forever"**
- **"Relationships are a waste of time"**
- **"Nothing good ever happens to me"**

What additional statements do you find yourself repeating time and time again based on your experiences (movies?)

Your task is not to seek for love, but merely to seek and find all the barriers within yourself that you have built against it – Rumi

WHAT'S BLOCKING YOU FROM LOVE?

It is crucial to ask yourself whether there is any benefit in keeping hold of limiting beliefs about love and relationships. It might seem like an odd question to ask. However, we often hold onto something that may limit us as it has a 'pay off' or secondary gain, a benefit of some sort. We may do this unconsciously without even realising it. More often than not, the things we say we don't want and don't like are things familiar to us. The feeling of familiarity and staying in our comfort zones can be appealing, even if we say we don't like it.

Power Questions

Think about the problem or limiting belief that you would like to change. Use the VoC Scale to measure the percentage of each belief and how true it is for you 0% being untrue and 100% being totally true for you.

You may wish to also start tapping round your tapping points as you ask yourself the following statements:

- **Do I deserve to get over this problem?**
- **Is it good for me to get over this problem?**
- **Is it safe for me to get over this problem?**
- **Is it safe for others if I get over this problem?**

- Is it possible for me to overcome this problem?
- Can I choose to allow myself to get over this problem?
- Am I willing to do what it takes to get over this problem?
- What are the negative aspects of you no longer having this problem?
- What would you lose if you didn't have this problem?
- What are the positive aspects of you not having this problem?
- What needs to happen to end this situation?
- What resources do you have or need to end this situation?

These additional phrases can be used to tap along to either by choosing the statement that you are most drawn to or working through the statements one by one.

- I deserve to get over this problem
- It is safe for me/others to get over this problem
- I am willing to do what it takes to get over this problem
- I will allow myself to get over this problem
- I am ready to get over this problem
- It is good for me to get over this problem
- It is possible for me to overcome this problem
- I benefit from getting over this problem
- Others benefit from me getting over this problem
- I have what it takes to get over this problem
- I choose to get over this problem
- I want to get over this problem

Byron Katie uses a very similar questioning process in her book 'Loving What Is', you might also like to explore her work as part of your ongoing personal journey of transformation.

You can only grow if you are willing to feel awkward and uncomfortable when you try something new – Brian Tracey

LEARNING ABOUT LOVE

At some point in your life, you would have learnt specific beliefs as they were passed down to you by family members or caregivers, or you would have formed your own love and relationship beliefs based on your own perceptions and experiences growing up and throughout your life. All fears come from the 'little you', the 'inner child' as it's sometimes referred to.

As children, we are like sponges soaking up information through all our senses, believing everything we are told by our parents and caregivers. We place meanings as we interpret   events and experiences and everything we learn is stored in the subconscious mind. We form beliefs about the world around us and about other people, including love and relationships.

Bruce Lipton, cell biologist explains the concept of this in his book Spontaneous Evolution: Our Positive Future and a Way to Get There from Here. I have paraphrased his account which details how the subconscious mind downloads information from the environment.

Before the age of six, while we are in what's called a 'hypnagogic' state literally hypnotised by all the information coming at us. Some of the beliefs, perceptions and inferences we form are untrue, our analytical self conscious mind doesn't fully exist and does not have the filters or discriminations that we develop after the age of six. We form beliefs based on what we 'assume' rather than what is fact. This often causes us problems later on in life, especially in the love and relationship area of our lives.

As adults, we hold onto those childhood beliefs, often without questioning where they came from, if they are/were true and if it is appropriate for us to hold onto them now. It's the beliefs we form about love and relationships at that age, which can become a patterns of behaviour that we default to for the rest of our lives. Our subconscious beliefs keep running until we explore what we believe and how that is showing up in our lives.

Some of you may remember reading a children's story book called Charlotte's Web by EB White, a classic line from this book is 'what a tangled web we weave'. In love and relationships, we weave a complicated web of stories about how love and relationships 'should or shouldn't be' based on our beliefs.

Our pre set expectations about love and relationships are based on beliefs, perceptions, judgements and also our need for love, approval and acceptance from others. We often hand over the responsibility of being loved to another person (acting as a child would) and that in itself can put huge pressure on relationships.

Not only do we lose a sense of our identity, we also give up on taking responsibility for ourselves to fulfil our own needs. It often becomes an obsession to get our needs met by others and when they are not met, the issue can feel as crucial as life or death!

As children growing up, it is natural for us to look towards our caregivers and parents to cater to our every whim, to seek for and be rewarded with love, approval, acceptance and nurturing, though as adults it becomes our personal responsibility to give those things to ourselves, It's no longer appropriate to look outside of ourselves for these things or to demand them in a relationship.

It is no longer appropriate as an adult to act from the 'little me' (your younger self/ inner child) where you may be coming across as a needy baby or demanding child. In fact it complicates matters if we are constantly clingy, needy and wanting to be 'filled up' with love, approval, acceptance or attention from another.

When we truly grow up and take full responsibility to heal old wounds and take care of our own needs, our lives can change dramatically. We have the capacity to totally transform them. Life becomes all that we imagined and more.

Case Study – Andy

I worked with Andy, a young man in his twenties who was newly married and unhappy in his relationship because his wife Sally didn't look after him or his home as well as his mum did when he was growing up. He formed the belief in childhood, seeing his mum care for him, his dad and brother, that 'wives should do all the cooking, cleaning, shopping and childminding'.

When we reflected on how different his mother's life was compared to his Sally's, he gained many insights. Firstly, Andy's mum was from a different era, was a full-time housewife, while his dad was the breadwinner. Andy's mum had the time she needed to cook, clean and nurture two young boys.

In comparison, Sally worked full time and was also helping Andy to run his business. Sally ran the home and was also busy looking after two young children. The relationship was hostile and challenging with both Andy and Sally feeling stressed, feeling unheard and unappreciated.

Andy came to see me because he was scared that his relationship would end and he would not be able to see his children who he adored, if his angry outbursts towards his family continued.

It was only after we explored Andy's past using The Spotlight Process that he realised his beliefs were outdated for this era, he realised that he had formed certain conditions about what he thought a wife should do and be. He became aware that he had formed a view based on the dynamics he saw around him growing up and he gained the insight that he expected Sally to look after him as his mother had.

Andy realised too that he felt unloved when his wife wasn't giving him what his mother had provided to him as a small boy.

After some self reflection and comparison between his life and that of his parents, he was aware that the belief was outdated and not transferable to his current situation and no longer appropriate for his marriage to develop and grow.

Andy used EFT in support sessions that we had together and also in between sessions when he felt stressed, angry and irritable.

Andy also made some practical changes after discussing with his wife what she needed help with. Andy hired a cleaner to help Sally at home, he asked his mother if she could look after his children once a month over a weekend to give the couple some 'adult time' and their relationship improved immensely just because he examined his beliefs using The Spotlight Process and worked through his own personal limitations from the past, outdated beliefs from childhood and the unexpressed overwhelming emotions he had been holding onto using EFT.

Last time I heard from Andy, he and Sally were looking to move home, the couple were communicating more effectively, they were 'back in love' and his anger was no longer a problem in the relationship. Andy's business is even more successful, as he is less stressed and is able to focus on his future and what he wants to achieve for himself and his family. Andy has also gone back to swimming through the week after work as a way of de-stressing and separating his work time and family time. In every area of Andy's life there has been improvement by simply applying and using The Spotlight Process and EFT.

As you read through the book, there will be key points in the questioning that I use and the information I share with you that will help you to examine your own beliefs, perceptions and judgements which will aid you to uncover the blocks that might be preventing you from finding love and enjoying happy and harmonious relationships.

When you have lost something in your life, stop thinking it was a loss for you...it's a gift you have been given so you can get to the right path to where you are meant to go, not where you think you should have gone - Suze Orman

Chapter 4

The Past

THE PAST

THE GOOD, THE BAD AND THE UGLY

When it comes to love, the past has a lot to answer for. We often replay in our minds, all of the negative aspects about love and relationships, seldom coming up for air about any of the positives and often telling the story about the unfairness of our circumstances and speaking from the point of view of victim.

I have been there myself expecting my future to be like my past was, until I woke up and realised that I can create my own reality. I do not have to let my past mould and shape my future and neither do you.

HOW IS YOUR THINKING LIMITING YOU?

It's my intention in this section to help you get clear about what thoughts may be limiting you and how those thoughts can be transformed into ones that are more positive and enabling for you. I will guide you to think about and explore your past and work with you to discover any mistakes that you feel you may have made knowingly or unknowingly, so that you have a new approach to finding and keeping love. I will support you as you shift the patterns and behaviours from your past, to create new and inspiring beginnings that leave you feeling more empowered and confident about life and love.

Many of our thoughts are automatic, unconscious and negative and we create rules for ourselves and others, which are often impossible to follow. The techniques shared with you in this book, will help you to identify any limiting core beliefs that may have been keeping love out of your life, so that you can go on to attract and bring into your life, the love and relationships that you may yearn for.

The following exercise and exploration questions, will guide you to discover any limiting thoughts and beliefs that you may have about love and relationships. You will be able to examine your answers and gain insight into why you may expect the worst possible outcome in future love and relationship ventures.

It will be helpful for you to list your negative beliefs about love and relationships, in order to further explore when they were formed and how long you have been holding on to these beliefs.

Be really honest with yourself and write uncensored, listing everything that's been festering in you, all the frustrations, unfairness, all the shames, doubts, worries and fears, including all the ugly stuff that you hoped would just go away and not keep on coming back and biting you on the bum!

Love relationships as they begin and end, go through different cycles and we experience many mixed emotions throughout. When a relationship ends, we go through the grieving process, even if that person hasn't died and maybe didn't even treat us particularly well. We still can grieve for the loss of all that we hoped for in our partners and the relationship.

Be gentle with yourself as you work through this book and any emotions that come up as you read through, just allow them to surface as they are an indication of what remains to be cleared and transformed using EFT. If you do need some support as you go along, I offer various programmes that will aid your progress.

 **Practical Exercise
(15 minutes)**

To explore your general beliefs about love and relationships, complete the statements below with your own ending in your journal (you may even have several endings based on how far your thinking reaches about each statement) and have additional statements that you would like to add to the list

- **All men/women/relationships are.....**
- **Good relationships are.....**
- **I always seem to attract people who.....**
- **My parents' beliefs about love and relationships are.....**
- **When I think about love I feel.....**
- **When I'm in a relationship I.....**
- **The thought of having a happy loving relationship makes me feel.....**
- **I tend to meet men/women who are.....**
- **When it comes to relationships I always.....**
- **If I met my life partner I'm afraid that.....**
- **Being in a loving relationship is.....**
- **You're better off alone because.....**

These statements offer further guidance to explore your thinking patterns when it comes to love and relationship fears.

LOVE= (I.e. love hurts, love means you lose yourself/self identity, love is painful, love is hard to find, love never lasts)

RELATIONSHIPS= (i.e. relationships are hard work, relationships don't last, good relationships are hard to find, you can't trust anyone, and all my relationships fail)

 Insightful Questions

- **Do you expect a relationship to last when you meet someone new, or is it already doomed from the start?**
- **Do you believe that new relationships will probably be like past relationships?**
- **Do you think love is unattainable or hard to find?**
- **Do you think that being in a relationship is hard work and not worth the effort?**
- **Are you confident in yourself and your lovability?**
- **How hopeful are you about having positive and loving relationships in the future?**

We all get into patterns of acting and responding that become so automatic and ingrained that we no longer even realise how we think and behave. By examining our thoughts, actions and behaviours we have the opportunity to change them into something far better.

Now is the right time to take full responsibility for your thoughts and reflect on how your negative expectations may have influenced patterns in your past relationships. There is no blame here, up to now you may have been projecting negative expectations into the future to try and keep yourself safe from hurt and pain. The things that we worry about often never happen, but if we continue to believe that they will, we are never able to experience a sense of wholeness, self belief or love.

I wish to guide you to a place of knowing that it is possible to change old thought habits and create new constructs to attract more of what you want and less of what you don't want.

Applying The Spotlight Process and EFT to your life, love and relationships, will open up new doors of possibility, whatever your situation and experiences. These two powerful techniques have helped hundreds of people to transform love and relationships opening up new doors of opportunity.

Rather than being your thoughts and emotions, be the awareness behind them-Eckhart Tolle

Spotlight on the Past

The only way out is through – John Bradshaw

Where to begin – Insightful Questions

- **How much of your past is affecting your life right now? Think about that for just a moment......**

- **How does your past influence your future?**

- **What thoughts, feelings and emotions are you experiencing regularly that are unpleasant and unwanted repetitions of the past?**

- **What scenarios are you playing out in your mind that are projections into the future - based on old, outdated memories or negative beliefs about how things will work out?**

- **Are you really living your life right now, or are you living in the past?**

- **What proportion of past negative thinking gets in the way from having the love and relationship you would like?**

- **When you think more positively about love and relationships, what does this give you?**

- **If you made the decision today to always operate from the place of love (thinking through the eyes of love, feeling love in your heart and filtering for love all around you) how will this make a difference to your future?**

Rest assured, nearly all of us get into habitual negative patterns of thinking at some time in our lives. It's a natural human response that when things don't go the way we want them to, we worry those exact same things will happen again. We try to keep ourselves safe from ever experiencing those things again and often this way of thinking will limit us as it may seem too scary to take risks.

The Spotlight Process will help to clarify how many of your thoughts are fear based stemming from a past negative experience, beliefs or perceptions.

When you are able to review your past as a learning experience taking with you the knowledge and wisdom gained from challenges, setbacks, wrong choices and perceived mistakes, it's possible to make your past work for you to your best advantage. Your past will no longer keep you in fear, terrified, doubtful, limited, trapped or anxious about the future.

When you can easily apply The Spotlight Process daily in your life and you begin to operate from a place of positive thinking about the best possible outcomes the future may hold for you this then becomes a winning formula to attract the love and relationships that you hope for.

It's natural, the way our minds work, to be afraid of certain things. Fear is, after all, a warning signal that we may be in danger, though often what we are afraid of or think will happen isn't a life and death scenario, it's just our mind preparing us for the worst possible event. Then, our minds escalate the belief of what we think will happen, in an attempt to prepare us for fight or flight. Our behaviours in the purest form are animalistic. When we are in fear, being open to love may appear 'too risky', 'too scary' or even 'terrifying'.

THE JOURNEY TO TRANSFORMATION

Being aware of your responses to real and imagined situations is part of the journey towards transformation.

When it comes to love and relationships for example it could be that a partner has cheated on you in the past and you believe that this will happen again in the future. Perhaps your significant other is going away for a weekend with friends, you may fear them not coming back home for certain reasons and you play these negative scenarios out in your mind. Maybe you also feel threatened by others who you believe to be more attractive than you and fear that you are not good enough when you compare yourself to others.

These examples break down to the fight, flight and freeze response, you may run and leave a relationship for fear of getting hurt before the other person has an opportunity to leave you, you may stay and fight with someone your partner might look at or talk to, you might go into freeze unable to do anything for yourself and become dissociated when your partner is away from you.

Sometimes, with all the catastrophic thinking that goes on inside our heads, it's rather like having a nagging parrot on your shoulder, following you around everywhere you go, saying 'you can't do this, you can't do that, it's too risky, too dangerous and too scary etc, it can't possibly work this time because it didn't last time, you should never even try that, you know the story don't you? This nagging voice goes on and on and on, talking you out of the very things that you say you want.

We are going to change that nagging parrot's voice to one that is encouraging. A voice that is supportive, kind and loving. A voice that will inspire you and that will remind you that you can do anything, be anything and have anything you want and more. A voice that you will pay attention to and listen to, as it has your best interests at heart.

''no matter what you're going through, there is a light at the end of the tunnel and it may seem hard to get to it but you can do it and just keep working towards it and you'll find the positive side of things'' Demi Loveto

**Practical Exercise
(15-20 minutes)**

Use this table to measure and track your own thought processes, being aware of when you escalate a triggered response, knowingly or unknowingly.

Trigger	What you say about the trigger	= energy block or lack of positive energy flow
Event as a trigger: *i.e. partner tells you they are going away with friends for the weekend*	**Event as a trigger:** *I.e. ''they don't love me, they will cheat on me, I'm not good enough''*	**Perception/Inference/beliefs create external and internal changes - physically and emotionally:** *I.e. panic, anxiety, fear, nausea, upset stomach, obsessive thoughts, anger, frustration, perception of loss*

Situation as a trigger: I.e. Boyfriend/ girlfriend looks at another attractive woman /man	Beliefs/perceptions/ inferences about the trigger I.e. He/she fancies them, he/she will leave me, I'm not pretty/sexy/slim enough etc	Perceptions and beliefs may create physical symptoms (racing heart, sweaty palms, headaches) I.e. anxious, hot, heart racing, angry, argumentative, accusing
Person as a trigger I.e. Ex husband/ Ex wife	The story that you are building up, talking about and re-experiencing related to the trigger I.e. He/she won't take care of the children, he's/ she's unreliable, can't be trusted, useless, stupid etc	When the story builds up we are reacting to the story (our thoughts and emotions about it) rather than the trigger itself I.e. panic, fear, not sleeping, lack of trust, accusation etc
Many things can trigger us via sensory channels Seeing/hearing/ feeling/smelling/ tasting	It's often not the trigger that we are responding to, but what we are saying about the trigger that affects us. It's the meaning or the belief that we infer that can often create additional problems	Our behaviour and our actions relate more to what we think is happening and the meaning we have placed on it, rather than what is actually happening

MORE ON THE PAST
AND HOW WE LEARN ABOUT LOVE

The past is where we learn about love, where we learn how to give love and how to receive love. It is in our early years that our identities concerning our lovability are formed. We soak up every piece of information around us through our senses and store this information in the retrieval system of our minds.

Our parents and caregivers are the people who teach us about love, based on what they know to be true and are formed through their own experiences of love.

We watch, listen and learn from our caregivers, their beliefs about love become our own beliefs (or, we may form totally different beliefs about love and relationships depending on the perceptions of events that we have experienced in our lives to date).

There is never any blame as to whether or not you felt unloved growing up as a child, the people who cared for you were doing the best that they could with the knowledge and experience they had at that time. They, too, had their own unique love needs that may or may not have been met by their own caregivers or with their own love and relationship experiences.

Think back to your past right now and reflect on the times where you may have felt that love was denied or withheld. Where love may have been conditional on how well you behaved. Where it appeared you had to compete for love (sibling rivalry, step family jealousy, family members being unwell and needing a lot of time and attention etc).

Love can feel like a struggle at times, a battle of sorts, a push pull of emotions, a whirlwind of thoughts and feelings that tug on our heart strings. We learn to protect ourselves from fear of rejection, recrimination, criticism or judgement.

GIVING AND RECEIVING LOVE

We can use love to manipulate others into doing things for us and offer more love in return (which again is conditional) if we feel our needs are being met. We may withdraw and withhold love as a punishment if we think our needs are being ignored. Love can be like a never ending seesaw of emotions and our love dial can go up and down, depending on the meaning we place on external situations, internal thinking and storytelling about a specific event, person or experience.

THE CHILD INSIDE

As children, we have our basic needs such as being fed, cared for, clothed and homed. Emotionally however, our needs are complex and extend far beyond the simple desire to be loved.

A baby requires attention, sensory stimulation, communication, affection (physical touch), a sense of safety and a secure emotional attachment and bonding with our parents or caregivers. These things are needed for a child's development and to build up a healthy mental foundation to be able to form strong, positive and secure relationships. This foundation influences how we behave as adults and shapes and forms our future and dictates how we respond to others and the world around us.

There are many childhood studies in this area. The Unicef Office of research documents - The United Nations Convention requires that ''children, including the very youngest children be respected as persons in their own right. Young children should be recognised as active members of their families, communities, societies, with their own concerns, interests and points of view" Distr.General CRC/C/GC/7 Rev.1. 20 September 2006

HOW WE ARE INFLUENCED AS CHILDREN

Our caregivers will be influenced by their culture, family of influence, religion, spirituality, media, their environment and perhaps many other aspects such as personal experiences, gender and not forgetting each parents' personal identity, self concept and overall level of self worth. It's natural for our parents to pass onto us their own influences, behaviours, values and beliefs, as this is what they hold true for themselves.

As children, we are often far more fragile than is realised and our sense of self can be shattered often by the words, actions and behaviours shown to us by our circle of influence (the circle of people around us) as we are growing up.

A child doesn't intuitively know that it's often their behaviour or actions that are unacceptable, unwelcome or challenging for the parent and when scolded or disapproved of, the child may think it's fundamentally 'them' that's bad, unloved, and unacceptable and disapproved of (and not their behaviour).

If love is conditional, given only as a reward for good behaviour, the child may often be in fear of being their unique selves and it may feel unsafe for them to reveal the full range of emotions that all children have.

HOW WE FORM OUR IDENTITY AND SENSE OF SELF WORTH

It's in our earliest years from birth to the age of two, that we develop our basic emotions such as happiness, interest, surprise, fear, anger and sadness. We are like sponges soaking up the emotions of others and learning from them about how to respond and behave.

From age two we form a sense of 'self'. Self worth and self identity are influenced by many factors. We are learning about our value and self worth as a person and our self concept which is developed by how others regard or treat us.

We develop the emotions of guilt, envy, pride, shame and embarrassment at this stage of development and we are aware of when we are scolded or being shown approval, affection and acceptance. It's at this time that we develop self-efficacy (the way we think about and motivate ourselves) and self-reliance, learning about persisting with tasks independently.

Our self-talk develops at this time, which impacts us negatively or positively,

depending on our internal dialogue and this in turn affects self esteem and self worth. We can often feel invalidated, disregarded and unloved without another's external approval, acceptance and love as we seek this constantly when growing up.

'LITTLE ME'

That 'Little Me' is developed, along with the inner misconceptions about the sense of self. The little me operates from this place throughout life, often only taking action when things seem certain and safe.

The 'little me' reacts all through adulthood and when it is re-triggered. It reacts not in this current moment, but from the place and time when our earliest emotional or physical needs were not being met by our care givers for whatever reason when we were children.

OUR EMOTIONAL NEED FOR SAFETY

Any emotions and feelings not acknowledged in childhood, may impact how we show up in the world as adults and we run a constant cycle of responding emotionally from the hurt place of our younger selves.

Every time we experience something that seems similar to that which we have already experienced, we feel an intensity of emotion that comes from the past and not wholly relevant to what is going on in the present moment. We have often reacted automatically to new experiences through old emotional filters. It's only with hindsight that it's possible to see that this is an old dynamic and an old pattern of responding.

Our emotions are so powerful. We use them to guard our basic needs and to keep ourselves safe. If we feel threatened in any way, our emotions signal to us and alert us to a perceived or real threat, the bottom line for us is survival in its barest form. We function from the fight flight or freeze response which is often disproportionate and unnecessary in terms of what we are reacting to.

If our unmet needs were never grieved for, if the beliefs that we formed were never questioned in relation to an actual experience and our emotions were not transformed, we would carry on with this cycle of behaving and reacting to the past with fears for our survival, instead of experiencing things in the present moment.

Guidance can be offered to the parent or caregiver through a variety of ways on how to raise children, though this advice may not take into account what has happened to the parent or caregiver in the past. Perhaps they never experienced for themselves love, acceptance, approval or acknowledgement. If they have received these things growing up themselves they do not know how to give these things to another.

Different experiences can result in different emotions and will shape how we respond to and fix or solve problems and overcome difficulties. We gauge what our personal qualities are, our strengths and our limitations from what we hear about ourselves growing up.

HOW OUR EARLY UPBRINGING DRIVES AND SHAPES OUR FUTURE

Our self identity affects our self worth and impacts our perceptions of others and indeed, we form judgements and misconceptions on how we are being perceived by them. The knowledge we have of ourselves may be built from false beliefs where we have inferred from others doubts about our capabilities.

There are many books on raising babies, children and teens and I do believe that each family is unique in the sense that every family will have its own set of beliefs, values and rules passed down through ancestry.

This historical blueprint (the characteristics of our body and mind) and genetic inheritance come from our ancestors. This blueprint can shape our abilities, mannerisms and physical features. We also receive through our time line, the emotions of our ancestors carried from their lifetime. If you find yourself plagued by emotions that seem to have no root in your life time, it might be interesting to look back at your ancestors for clues.

EMOTIONS IN THE WOMB

Something else to consider is how 'in vitro,' in the womb, emotions are being picked up by the child from the mother. This will include how she feels generally, her experience of pregnancy, emotions that relate to her relationship with the father, the father's presence too if he is with the expectant mother, will all contribute to the environmental factors that may be influencing the mother and child. The way the mother cares for herself in pregnancy and her emotional wellbeing, also influences the child's development physically and emotionally.

How we react to today, may also be as a result of how we felt as a child in the womb. If our mothers were anxious and afraid during pregnancy or if she was unhappy about being pregnant or had a difficult pregnancy and birth, we too may feel unhappy or anxious with the belief of 'the world is not a safe place.'

I'd like to share this case study with you to highlight how our early upbringing drives and shapes our future.

Case Study – Jenny

Jenny was born into the world with alcoholic parents, her mother was in and out of psychiatric care. Life was very chaotic growing up and Jenny spent periods of time in and out of foster care. Life, love and relationships for most of Jenny's young life were traumatic. Years would go by when she never saw her mother; her father had affairs and introduced her to 'new aunties', none behaving as Jenny's desired mother figure as they were not able to show her the love, time and care that she craved. It was hard for Jenny to trust that love was possible as she had closed off the idea that she was lovable. Jenny felt incredibly lonely, confused and neglected for much of her early life and it was hard for her to realise that despite this, she was in fact worthy of being loved by another.

Working with Jenny using The Spotlight Process we explored where her fears came from. Nothing was certain growing up for her and she believed that men were unreliable, could not be trusted not to cheat on women and that love was unreliable. Jenny had a fear that love would be taken away as her own mother was taken away many times into psychiatric care, she never knew when her mum would return and was not allowed to see her mum in hospital. Her needs as a child were not met adequately enough for her to form positive beliefs about love and relationships in later life.

Jenny was reluctant to believe she would find lasting love and was scared of taking risks. She wanted very much to be in a relationship and to have her own children; so that she could give to them the love that she felt she never had growing up

We worked together using EFT to clear the unhappy and traumatic memories from the past. We worked through low self-esteem issues and also transformed the grief and loss of not having the kind of parents that she would have liked to have had. We worked on forgiveness of her parents, so that Jenny could set herself free from the heartache of her past and also acknowledge that it was not her fault that she did not receive the love and care that she needed growing up. Jenny was able to resolve and work through many layers of built up emotions using The Spotlight Process and EFT and the change in Jenny's confidence, self worth and self esteem was amazing. Her feedback to me in an email was "I wake up every day now believing in myself".

Jenny contacted me recently to say that she had got back in touch with a childhood sweetheart and to tell me that she has been dating him for some time and that they are living together and planning to get married. Jenny's sense of self love had grown immensely, she said she believed that now she could do anything she set her mind to. Jenny had learnt to love herself first, to look after her own needs, rather than be dependent on another to provide what she can provide for herself. She no longer rejects herself or feels unloved, if her fiancé goes away for a weekend or is home late, she trusts fully and completely that she is a wonderful person worth loving, regardless of how others behave or act towards her. She knows and believes fully that she is lovable and worthy of love.

Jenny has come such a long way, she has blossomed into a wonderful woman. She has let go of the emotions she had been carrying with her from the past and now focuses fully on the future and all that is possible for her.

LOVE AND EMOTIONAL BONDING
ARE KEY INFLUENCERS FOR OUR SURVIVAL

We form beliefs based on survival instincts in their barest form. When we think that love is being denied, taken away from us, or based on conditional love, we think that we cannot live without love so our survival instincts and the fight and flight mode kick in.

Love is what we are born with, fear is what we learn – Marianne Williamson

TAKE A MOMENT TO REFLECT ON YOUR LOVE RELATIONSHIPS

The love and relationship inventory is designed to bring clarity to your love and relationship experiences and beliefs. As you read through the inventory, answer honestly if the statements resonate with you.

While completing this you will gain insights into whether you are needy and dependent in a relationship, or if you are authentic and autonomous.

There is no blame here, somewhere along the line you would have learnt beliefs and behaviours that meant you put love and self worth outside of yourself. There may have been times through your life experiences where you have felt unworthy, unloved and rejected, though if this has been your experience in the past, there is no evidence that history will repeat itself, except for your thinking making it so.

You may find that some statements overlap and you might waiver between different answers for different kinds of relationships (relationships with a significant other, relationships with a parent or child, relationships with friends and colleagues). You may even notice that you behave the same way in all relationships and that you I seek approval, acceptance and love from outside of yourself across a wide variety of relationship experiences.

If, as you read through the questions, you are aware of an emotional charge related to any of the statements, then please use EFT to clear whatever comes up for you. You can work through each statement and the different aspects that apply to you.

Use the statements the same way you would The Spotlight Process as a guiding light to get clear on what you need to change about your perceptions and beliefs and how you view love and relationships.

It's natural when you explore love and relationships that all sorts of thoughts, feelings and emotions could raise to the surface, some good and some not so good. Being open to any emotions that come up and simply noticing those emotions and identifying the emotion (i.e. anger, frustration, guilt, rage etc) means that it is there to be resolved.

Emotions are a record of the past in their own right and there to help us, not to harm us, it just depends on how we view the emotion as to whether we use it to limit us or help us to grow from the experience of feeling this emotion. All unresolved emotions have the potential to be transformed using EFT.

EFT is an ongoing process and can be used not only as a resource to aid your own growth and transformation while reading this book, but also as a resource to empower you in the future. Once you have learnt this technique, I suggest applying it to work through challenges from the past including as and when life events happen.

LOVE AND RELATIONSHIP INVENTORY

 Insightful Questions

- **Read through the statements below and make a note of the ones that you agree with**

- **Use this section as a guiding light to bring awareness to what you would like to change for yourself. As you read through, score the intensity of your emotions related to each statement, using the SUD (Subjective Unit of Distress) Scale**

- **To measure the how true a limiting belief may be for you, you can also scale the percentage of how true your belief is. The VoC scale (Validity of Cognition) measures your current self limiting beliefs rating them from a 0 when you have no belief at all to 100 when the belief feels completely true for you**

- What you find yourself agreeing with may be a limiting belief. The limiting beliefs will need to be explored to pinpoint where the belief came from and if the belief is still appropriate for you right now as an adult. Keep a note of any limiting beliefs connected with each statement.

- If the beliefs that you identify with are limiting you apply EFT and you will soon notice the release you feel from working through those feelings.

- I appreciate that there are a lot of statements here. Read through them all and to be really honest as you answer each point, as this will bring awareness to the areas of your love and relationship beliefs that may need to be cleared, transformed and evolved using EFT, so that you realise who you are is lovable - in or out of a relationship.

- Use EFT to reduce the emotional charge around your beliefs and any remembered experiences triggered by these statements. If you are able to link back to your earliest memory of when the statement became relevant for you, this will be more effective than working on more recent events and relationships.

- You may find it helpful to explore the love and relationship beliefs of your parents and caregivers, as it's possible that some of the beliefs that you are running are, in fact, their beliefs that have been handed down to you and learnt from them based on their own experiences of love and relationships.

**Practical Exercise
(20 minutes)**

Love and Relationship Inventory	SUD	VOC
I have a preconceived vision of love and relationships and how they 'should' be		
Love needs to be a certain way for me to be happy		
I offer love based on conditions		
I believe that love can only be experienced by receiving it from another		
I think it's selfish to love myself		
I question and judge the actions of others instead of being in the flow of love		
I spend time worrying that I'm not getting enough love		

I believe that the past will repeat itself and I'm scared of getting hurt		
I put love outside of myself rather than taking responsibility to give love to myself		
I believe that if I love someone, their love may be stolen or taken away from me		
I believe I am unlovable or unworthy of love		
I lose my self identity when I'm in a relationship		
If I love again I fear being rejected		
I expect love to be like one of the fairy tales I read as a child		
I gain my self-worth and value through others		
My sense of security is only present when I'm in a relationship		
I am dependent on others for love		
Other people have better relationships than me		
I don't know how to love myself		
I end relationships before I have given them a chance to blossom		
I sabotage my future hopes by not having a relationship and 'playing safe'		
I put other people's feelings ahead of my own		
I need to be loved to feel complete		
I want to be close to someone but I'm afraid of being vulnerable		
It feels scary to open up to another person and be intimate		
It feels safer to be out of a relationship than in one		
I don't know who I am outside of a relationship		
My happiness depends on being in a relationship		
My emotional wellbeing depends on another person's validation of me		
I feel like a 'nobody' unless somebody loves me		
I am desperate to be loved		
I will not give my love unless I get 100% love back from the other person		
When I don't get what I want from a relationship I feel cheated and let down		
I try to change the people I am in a relationship with		
When a relationship ends I feel like a failure		
When I'm by myself I don't feel like a complete person		
I feel empty and alone when I'm not in a loving relationship		
I am preoccupied by negative relationships from the past		
Without a relationship my life would be empty and meaningless		
I'm frightened of being alone for the rest of my life		
I can't stand on my own two feet without someone to lean on		
If I'm in a relationship I'm on alert and expect things to go wrong		
I have never got what I wanted from relationships		

I look for evidence that I'm unlovable		
When I'm in a love relationship I look for all the flaws in my partner and the relationship itself		
I cling to hopes and dreams of a relationship working out, even though I know it's best for me to leave		
I don't seem to exist outside of a relationship		
I go into relationships blindly, it's better to be in one than alone		
I often feel alone and unhappy when I'm in a relationship		
I need to build myself up by making others love me		
I look for signs that my relationships will not work out		
It feels unsafe for me to be totally me and share all of myself in a relationship		
I drift from relationship to relationship, I have never spent time alone		
In relationships I become totally dependent on the other person to provide my happiness		
I go into relationships for the wrong reasons		
There must be something wrong with me if I'm not in a relationship		
I constantly think about negative experiences in previous relationships		
I feel like I can't move on from negative relationships from the past		
I put all my energy into my relationship and leave nothing for me		
I'm afraid that I will never be loved		
I feel insignificant and worthless outside of a relationship		
Life only has meaning if I'm in a relationship		
I feel more real in a relationship		
I need someone else to complete me		
I feel incomplete or off balance when I'm not in a relationship		
I don't trust anyone enough to share my feelings openly		
I am afraid of being honest or assertive in relationships		
I fear the physical or verbal violence that relationships can sometimes bring		
I am afraid that I will have to give up my family, career, hobbies etc if I have a relationship		
I put my own needs last in a relationship		
I find it hard to communicate my needs in a relationship		
I don't know who I am or what I want in a relationship		
I put up with unacceptable behaviour and hope that the other person will change		
I fear really being me, in case I'm not accepted, disapproved of, or rejected		

EMOTIONS ARE A RECORD OF THE PAST IN THEIR OWN RIGHT AND THERE TO HELP US, NOT TO HARM US

There are two basic motivating forces: fear and love. When we are afraid, we pull back from life. When we are in love, we open all that life has to offer with passion, excitement, and acceptance. We need to learn to love ourselves first...in all our glory and our imperfections. If we cannot love ourselves, we cannot fully open to our ability to love others or our potential to create. – John Lennon

COMFORT ZONE

Our comfort zone includes all the things that we are comfortable and familiar with - even if we don't like them. When we are in this zone we take no risks,   we are stagnating as we are not growing or evolving and we are just getting by.

Our comfort zone operates as a self protection mechanism and although we say that we want positive change we still stay in this zone, although it might be comfortable it can be compared to being trapped inside a cage too frightened to move out of it even if the cage door is open.

Consequently, the love that we search for is often slower to obtain, or there is no change at all if we stay stuck where we are. It's as though this invisible comfort zone is made up of a million voices telling us why we shouldn't, mustn't, ought not to, daren't, don't want to do whatever it is we say we really want to do.

ARE YOU STAYING IN YOUR COMFORT ZONE?

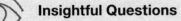 **Insightful Questions**

- **Has life been consistently knocking you down that as soon as you get up, you feel as if you're being pulled back down again?**
- **Has it been too scary for you to take risks that could lead you to the love you have been searching for?**
- **Have you been using your past to motivate you or limit you?**
- **How long have you been staying in the safety of your comfort zone?**

Anything outside of this zone can appear scary, risky or downright dangerous and our survival instincts kick in. Fear and excitement are so similar in the way we experience the feelings, that we may be uncertain which one we are feeling and so talk ourselves out of doing certain things. It's natural to feel apprehensive when trying new things, but unless we take action, nothing will change.

Mistakes, or rather the fear of making mistakes and not getting things 100% right, create a comfort zone.

A comfort zone consists of mental conditioning that may not always be based on fact and has been made up of our perceptions and the meanings we have placed on things and people. If we feel we have taken risks before and those risks have not worked in our favour, we may be hesitant to take risks again in case it all goes wrong.

CREATING OUR OWN PRISONS

The truth is, if we stay within the boundaries of the self-imposed walls we build up around ourselves, change won't happen - we'll be doing what we always did and getting the same results, feeling stuck, uncertain and unafraid.

By thinking and doing the same things, we get the same results. I don't really need to tell you that as I know you are already fed up with getting the same results.

MOVING ON FROM THE PAST AND CREATING THE FUTURE OF OUR DREAMS

So, it's time to join me and the hundreds of women I have worked with and form a united army moving on from the past and creating the future of our dreams. Focus on all that could go right and take those first steps towards achievement.

Life begins at the end of your comfort zone – Neal Donald Walsch

Case Study – Sandra

When Sandra came to see me, she was feeling desperate and lonely she had two young children and very little disposable income. She felt that life was passing her by and although she wanted to be in a new relationship, she feared being rejected again. Sandra had been in several unhappy relationships, her own upbringing had been confusing as she didn't know who her dad was, she had lots of flings with men hoping that each would be 'the one' but all she found at the end of each brief encounter there was nothing but disappointment and regret.

We explored Sandra's relationship behaviours, her beliefs about men in general and her hopes and dreams for the future. Sandra realised that although she said she wanted to be in a loving relationship underneath it all she had no respect for men and didn't believe that any man would stay for long, as this was her experience of her own father leaving when she was a baby. Her limiting beliefs about men were further compounded by her husband leaving her and other short term relationships she had, where the men she was choosing weren't emotionally available for her, or who would not stick around long enough to form a lasting and loving relationship.

Sandra had been meeting perspective partners at bars and clubs, when she and the men she was meeting were drunk. Sandra openly admitted to having the beer goggles on, she was so desperate to be loved that anyone who paid attention to her she automatically 'fell in love with' or, perhaps, we could say 'in lust'. It was never on Sandra's agenda to get to know someone as a person, before she became intimate with them, she honestly thought that this was the way relationships were formed as she had seen this pattern growing up with her mum who would introduce Sandra to different 'uncles' and bringing home lots of different men when she was a child.

Sandra worked though many unresolved emotions such as anger, rejection, fear, loss, low self esteem and worked through her core belief that she wasn't good enough. She stopped blaming the men who had left in the past, she forgave her mother for not knowing who her father was and as a result took responsibility for how she was showing up in the world.

Sandra learnt a lot about herself using The Spotlight Process and EFT, she realised how her own behaviour had impacted her relationships. It dawned on her that she had gone from relationship to relationship unconsciously, trying to fill the gap in her life left by not knowing who her father was and whether or not he loved her or would have wanted her if he had known about her.

Sandra put many ghosts from the past to rest and in doing so there was a lot of peace for her. She transformed her past using EFT, working through and transforming old memories and beliefs that she had been holding on to. Sandra decided to change the way she went about meeting a life partner and joined a dating site so that she could clearly define what kind of relationship she would like and the type of man she wanted to spend her future with. She chose to have coffee dates instead of bar dates, so that both she and any potential suitors were sober. In doing so, she began to break away from old behaviours.

I'm happy to share with you that since our work together, Sandra has been happily married for over five years after meeting Kevin, her husband, on-line., He is a tender and considerate man who has helped Sandra to bring up her two children as his own. She has shared with him details about her past and he has done the same with her and together they work through any challenges that come up, using EFT and The Spotlight Process.

They make a fantastic team and support each other lovingly and openly and can detect when either one has slipped back into the past, reacting from an old place of hurt or when they have jumped ahead into the future projecting negative outcomes. It's wonderful to see how couples can learn and use these simple techniques, so they can support each other to evolve further as individuals in their own right and also as a couple.

I love a happy ending and you too can achieve this for yourself when you start to use the past to work for you rather than against you.

Changing how you remember your past and using it as a motivating force, a fountain of strength and energy to overcome any setbacks, you too can make positive changes in your life.

If you want something in life that you've never had, you'll have to do something that you've never done – JD Houston

OLD OUTDATED MOVIES AND HOW WE REMEMBER THINGS

If I asked you to name your top three favourite movies, I bet you would be able to tell me about them straight away. The characters, the story line, the emotions that come up for you watching the film, where you first saw the film and who you were with. Memorable movies have a place in our hearts, and when we talk about why we love those particular movies so much, we re-experience watching the film for the first time. We may experience a sense of euphoria filling us up, lightness, hope and a sense of joy.

HOW WE STORE INFORMATION THROUGH OUR SENSES

We store information through our senses and just talking about what is remembered from the movie will re-trigger how you have stored that movie in sensory terms. You may remember what you saw vividly, what you heard with clarity and your favourite lines from the film, what you felt experientially watching it.

As an example, you may remember how you felt watching a love story where the hero and heroine have a happy ending or perhaps one partner dies. Or you remember a comedy that made you split your sides and cry with laughter, or an action film that got the heart racing and the blood pumping through your body or, perhaps a horror film that scared you and kept you awake at night.

In the same way, every time you replay your own personal movies, be aware that the thoughts, feelings and emotions you have, are all on replay and you may experience emotions that are fearful or terrifying. As well as remembering the movies that make you happy, your mind stores all of your life's experiences as if they were films, you have a storehouse of information within you that you will recall consciously and unconsciously.

THE MEANING WE PLACE ON OUR EXPERIENCES

Many years ago I studied NLP (Neuro Linguistic Programming) an approach to communication, personal development and psychotherapy which was created by Richard Bandler and John Grindler. Studying NLP helped me understand the way the mind works, how we store and retrieve information and how we communicate.

The mind is amazing, it's a storehouse of information that we filter through, judging new experiences through an old lens. We distort, delete and generalise experiences based on what's happened in previous 'movies'. We often predict how something will end even when we have no evidence, we just go back to an old movie that's similar in some way to the new experience and evaluate it through comparison with the record we already have.

**OUR PAST EXPERIENCES INFLUENCE
HOW WE REACT TO OTHERS AND THE WORLD AROUND US**

We often get things totally confused and what is actually happening may not even be recognised, as we have jumped back into default mode where we are basing current experiences that compare to similar ones that we have experienced in the past.

Our past experiences influence how we react to others and the world at large and also determine how we act and behave.   An external event will be experienced through our senses and before we make an internal representation of the event we filter the event.   We literally go inside that storehouse of information deleting, distorting and generalising the information through our five senses.

OUR STOREHOUSE OF SENSORY INFORMATION

- **Visual** (what we see outwardly, including how someone may look at us)

- **Auditory** (what we hear, including sounds, the words that we hear and the way words are spoken by others including tone and pitch)

- **Kinaesthetic** (what we feel internally inside our bodies or externally via touch, including the texture of something and level of pressure felt physically)

- **Gustatory** (taste)

- **Olfactory** (smell)

Deletion: When we delete information, we may be paying attention only to certain aspects of a situation and delete other aspects overlooking, ignoring and omitting sensory information coming into us. We delete in this way as there is so much information coming into us, that if we didn't delete we would experience too much sensory stimulation (information overload).

Distortion: It's easy to misrepresent reality. What is actually happening in an experience can be distorted and we can perceive things incorrectly. We distort, creating imaginary futures often in a negative way.

Generalisation: We can make up and form our beliefs based solely on one or two experiences. We absorb information and make assumptions about what the information means, comparing it to the information that we have already stored. Sometimes our assumptions are incorrect.

Insightful Questions

Use these questions to reveal what you may be distorting, generalising and deleting as you process information

- **What aspects of your relationships to you delete?** E.g. perhaps your partner takes out the rubbish and mows the lawn but does not say they love you or take you for meals, deleting what someone does do for you which may to them be a loving action can put pressure on a relationship if what they are doing isn't recognised. Spend some time noticing what others already do for you and you might be surprised and how much they do, do

- **How do you distort information that you are receiving in your relationship?** E.g. your husband/wife wants to go on a stag or hen weekend with friends, do you immediately think they are going to be unfaithful to you?

- **When do you generalise negatively about love and relationships?** E.g. men/women are all the same, everyone will let you down, no one is worth it etc

My past has not defined me, destroyed me, deterred me or defeated me, it has only strengthened me – Steve Maraboli

WHAT DO YOU SAY WHEN YOU TALK TO YOURSELF?

You may have noticed that you have a voice inside your head that sometimes whispers very gently to you words of encouragement, acknowledgement and praise, words of comfort, care and understanding. Words of support and tenderness though, more often than not, the second you have your back turned that voice may bellow, cagoule, ridicule and remind you of your faults , your inadequacies and may nag you at times, seldom coming up for air.

I like to call my voices **'The Voice of Doom'** and **'The Voice of Love'.** Do you have names for yours?

That negative inner voice may criticise you, judge you, compare you and tell you you're not good enough, worthy enough, capable enough or strong enough. Worse than that, it may even call you names or swear at you.   It may keep you tied to the belief that you're not lovable, that relationships cause pain and opening your heart to love is too risky.

Your voice is with you morning, noon and night, it can turn on the charm or pull the rug out from under your feet until you have a word with it and rein it in. That voice is with you at every stage of your life, every decision you make, every crossroads you face, every choice and every venture is dictated by that voice. Everyone has an internal voice, an endless stream of chatter a narrator talking you through your waking moments and through your dreams as well!

CONFRONTING AND QUESTIONING THE VOICE OF DOOM

Name your own voices and identify them as characters, the voices you may in fact know, they may be the voice of your parents, teachers, people you have lost contact with or a combination of internalised voices merging together, these voices are in fact just thoughts.

**Creative Practical Exercise
(15 minutes)**

Draw your voices (your versions of the voice of doom and the voice of love) in your journal or on pieces of paper.

Find a way to record the voices as characters perhaps sketching them or you may like to make a collage of how the voices look.

It's been interesting in my work to see my clients drawing their characters, changing the voices of the characters in their heads and also naming and shaming the voice of doom.

There is a stark contract between the voice of love and the voice of doom, one often an ugly scribble, a monster or a mess. The voice of love gentle, flowing and beautiful.

ADDING HUMOUR TO THE PROBLEM

That critical inner voice doesn't have the same impact when you turn it into a cartoon voice, speed up or slow down the voice. It's very cathartic to get a grip on the voices and realise that you control them, they don't control you. Adding humour to the voice of doom changes the impact it has on you.

The voice of doom you may be familiar with as it's often the louder of the two voices in your head. It's the voice that holds you back, the voice that takes you down and holds you tight in the grip of fear. It has a detective like persona that will only look for and gather together all the negatives it can about why love and relationships are

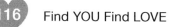

ill fated, impossible, too risky, and too scary. This voice will do little to encourage you to be open to the love, hope, joy and connection which having a positive relationship can bring.

THE PURPOSE OF THE CRITICAL VOICE

You may have found your voice of doom likes keeping you in your comfort zone where everything is safe and familiar; it shelters you from perceived threats, from the risk of harm, from danger, it is on the lookout, constantly gathering information to support the negative beliefs that you hold about yourself, other people and the world around you.

The voice of doom actually has a positive intention and what's beneath its harshness is a form of protection and tries to keep you safe from perceived risks to your survival.

Your internal dialogue was formed as part of your life experience from childhood to today. Every voice you have ever heard will become part of your own inner landscape and contribute to how you talk to yourself in moments of joy and moments of stress.

Knowing that the negative voice is really there to try and protect you gives a different meaning to it. As adults we can reflect on whether or not we listen to that voice or simply thank it for trying to watch out for us and then make our decisions based on the facts of a situation.

"We were born with love, fear is something we learn" Marianne Williamson

THE VOICE OF LOVE

The voice of love comes from deep within, from the very heart of you, from your intuition or what some may call higher wisdom (or gut feeling) from the very core of your being, the voice that was part of you when you were born, open to love, open to receiving, open to joy and possibility.

TAKING BACK YOUR POWER

Once you start to listen to this voice you have the potential to transform your life. You will be looking through the eyes of love, filtering for opportunity and open to receiving love. You will move to a place where anything seems possible and you welcome the unknown whatever it brings. We can never quantify everything, sometimes we just have to take a leap of faith, find our wings and fly.

The job of the voice of love is to keep you true to who you really are, to allow the essence of who you are to flow through, it's there to guide you towards happiness and love if you will stop and listen.

The voice of love may have been waiting in the wings for decades waiting to be heard. Allow it to step forward, to welcome it with open arms, listen to it and trust and respect that this voice needs some air space too.

BREATHE LIFE INTO THE VOICE OF LOVE

Listening to this voice, connecting with it at times of indecision, will serve you well. Ask yourself **"what would love do here?"** and then let the voice of love (your inner voice) express itself. This is the voice of your inner power, the truth of who you are.

The voice of love can be compared to a gentle voice perhaps caring for and speaking with a two year old, calming and soothing them, being patient, loving and forgiving.

Now that you understand more about your negative internal voice and its intention you can decide if it's time to stop listening to the voice of doom, because there is another way – to listen only to the voice of love.

 Insightful Questions

Read through the following questions. Begin to notice which voice you pay attention to the most, notice how your emotions change based on which voice you listen to:

- **What voice have you been paying more attention to - the voice of doom or the voice of love?**

- **Does one or the other voice get louder when you're with certain people or in a certain place?**

- **Think about the tone of voice and what it says, who does this remind you of?**

- **What type of things do your voices say the most often to you?**

- **How has listening to the voice of doom affected you and your life to date?**

- **What opportunities have you missed out on by listening to the voice of doom?**

- **What can you put in place today to be sure that you listen more to the voice of love and less to the voice of doom?**

- **How can listening to the voice of love improve your life, love and relationships?**

LET LOVE BE THE ANSWER

We want the voice of love to stay within us at all times with a happy and loving commentary.

You may also wish to draw or find a symbol for the voice of love and know that it is within you at all times. Acknowledging the voice of love, listening to it, honouring it, respecting it and believing in it will change the way you feel about yourself.

The primary cause of our unhappiness is never the situation but the thought about it –Eckhart Tolle

FORGIVENESS

Forgiveness releases you from the past that no longer defines you, allow yourself to move on – Cheryl Richardson

Forgiveness will set you free from the past, it is essential to your personal growth and wellbeing.

The act of forgiveness sets you free from the negative energy you are holding onto. Without forgiveness, we are not completely whole, as part of us remains split off in the past.

Holding onto the emotions, thoughts and feelings connected with not forgiving an action, word or deed by someone else, means that we suffer.

THE PRICE WE PAY FOR NOT FORGIVING

Not forgiving, means that we are still connected to that person/event or situation and we keep the story alive, as if it were happening in this very moment.

Perhaps you may also need to forgive yourself for past actions, words and deeds? The emotions that we may have, such as anger, frustration, guilt, resentment or hatred, will fester and grow inside us unless we can transform them.

We are only hurting ourselves by holding onto these emotions when we choose not to forgive ourselves or others. Our hearts and minds become hardened, we operate from a victim mode and the energy of feeling like a victim may spill over into all areas of our lives; we stay inside the pain, the injustice, inside the prison of hurt, inside the grief and despair, locked into the past, frozen in time.

Forgiving means that you care about yourself enough to unlock yourself from the prison of your thoughts, feelings and emotions. Forgiving puts you in control, it releases the pain and sets you free, free to live the life that you dream of and deserve.

 Insightful Questions

Work through your own forgiveness process using these questions as an insight into your underlying emotions.

- **What does forgiveness mean to you?**
- **Have you ever forgiven anyone?**
- **Has anyone ever forgiven you?**
- **Do you need to forgive yourself for something?**
- **What is the cost of not forgiving yourself or others?**
- **What emotions do you hold onto when you choose not to forgive?**
- **How do these emotions limit you?**
- **What would you need to stop doing in order to forgive?**
- **What would you need to start doing in order to forgive?**
- **Is there someone who forgiving would benefit you?**
- **What are some of the personal benefits that you would gain from moving on from the past and forgiving, in order to set yourself free?**

I have worked with many people over the years, who have held onto their anger, grudges, hatred, spite, injustice, jealousy, and fear because of something that happened in their past. The thought of forgiving someone I realise, may evoke many emotions for you, as it's often thought that by forgiving someone it means that you agree with what they said or did. This is not the case.

FORGIVENESS, RELEASES ANY INTERNAL NEGATIVE ENERGY TOWARDS OURSELVES AND ANY EXTERNAL NEGATIVE ENERGY TOWARDS OTHERS.

Forgiveness sets you free. Forgiveness sets you free to live the rest of your life on your terms, you will feel more balanced and in control of your life.

Forgiveness gets you past the past so that you can live your life fully in the now

Forgiveness gives you the opportunity to choose your thoughts, reactions and outcomes, based on what you want, not what you don't want. Forgiveness gives you the wings to fly free and gives you the ability to let go of the hurt, the pain, the turmoil and bitterness that you may have been holding onto.

Forgiveness will allow you to blossom and to be open to all that is possible for you and more. Forgiveness gets you past the past, so that you live your life in the now.

FORGIVENESS IS THE GREATEST GIFT WE CAN GIVE TO OURSELVES

Forgiveness is the path to personal freedom. Forgiveness, as well as love, is the greatest gift we can give to ourselves. Once you are able to let go of past hurts, you will feel liberated, no longer a victim of the past. There is much freedom and joy when we choose peace.

Forgiveness releases negative energy within you and frees you to be more loving in the future. It's such a healthy choice to make, enabling you to be free to live the life you deserve on your terms.

The act of forgiving, does not mean that you have to contact the person; the forgiveness just takes place within you at a soul/energy level.   For every person you forgive, you will feel better about yourself and you will have more energy for love and living.

It will be interesting to explore who from your past you may consider forgiving, so that you are finally free to live the life you want and are no longer a prisoner to the past, or to the pain and hurt that may be present in you by not forgiving.

Forgiveness could relate to something someone did, said, or how they behaved towards you. If this exercise is difficult for you, start by forgiving yourself for not wanting to forgive! This includes accepting the emotions that go with that and focussing on each separate emotion using EFT, until the emotional intensity decreases.

EFT Practical Exercise
(open ended time frame)

Use the following scenarios as you apply EFT to:

- **Past hurts from childhood**
- **Disappointing relationships growing up**
- **Times of emotional challenge in adulthood**

Simply tap through all of your points, speaking out loud or inside your own mind the following statements, to include the name of the person you want to work towards forgiving.

- **I forgive myself for not wanting to forgive** 'name of person here'.....

- **Even though it's hard to forgive** 'name of person here' **I'm working towards forgiving him/her so that I can be free**

- **I might be able to forgive.....**

- **I could probably forgive.....**

- **I could someday forgive.....**

- **I could consider forgiving.....**

- **There is a possibility that I could forgive.....**

- **I might be able to forgive** 'name of person here' **someday**

- **Maybe I could let go of not forgiving.....**

- **Maybe** 'name of person here' **was just doing the best that they could and I forgive him/her/them**

- **Maybe I could forgive** 'name of person here' **so that I become free**

- **Maybe I could forgive myself for.....** (e.g. my choices, my own mistakes, my actions, my behaviours)

- **Maybe I didn't know any better and I forgive myself for.....**

- **I'm not agreeing with what** 'name of person here' **said/did though I choose to forgive them, so that I can be free from hurting myself with this memory**

- **I no longer want to be a prisoner in this memory and I choose forgive-**

ness now.....

- **Forgiveness means letting go of the past and I choose that for myself right now.....**
- **I choose to forgive.....**
- **I am willing to forgive.....**
- **I forgive** 'name of person here' **right now**

If you have been holding on to anger, resentment, hatred and pain or any other intense and limiting emotion that has stopped you from forgiving applying EFT will work towards reducing the emotional intensity of those unresolved emotions.

After going through the process of forgiving using EFT, you may feel a little empty as the negative energy of not forgiving, leaves our body.

RECLAIMING LOVE

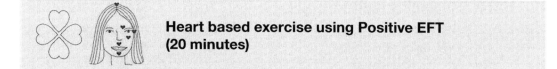

Heart based exercise using Positive EFT (20 minutes)

After working through the forgiveness exercise, think about what your heart needs to replace the empty space. If it's more love that you need, then give that to yourself. Go back to the Positive EFT section and apply this process now.

You'll never see the great things ahead of you if you keep looking at the bad things behind you. You are exactly where you need to be to reach your goals. Everything you've been through was preparation for where you are right now and where you can be tomorrow – Melchor Lim

TRANSFORM YOUR PAST USING EFT

Think about all the reasons why forgiving, letting go of the past and setting yourself free could benefit you.

Just like clearing out a wardrobe that has been full of outdated clothes that are no longer a good fit for you, they are worn out and falling apart. It's also possible for you to throw out old, outdated thinking and make space for the new, fresh and vibrant choices that there may be no room for otherwise.

If you were to count, every day, how many of your negative thoughts relate to the past, I do believe you would surprise yourself!

Case Study – Paula

Paula at the age of forty three, was struggling to hold down a long term relationship, she would allow herself to get close to someone and then pull back, often ending the relationship before it really began to blossom. She had many friendships with men and lots of events to attend socially, group outings, parties and work socials, though she didn't know what was stopping her from wanting to get more involved. Just as she got close to upping her game and getting closer to someone and making a commitment, she pulled back.

Working with Paula and utilising The Spotlight Process taught her so much about herself. On the outside, she appeared confident, chatty, vivacious, attractive and happy but inside; she was shy, nervous and felt quite vulnerable around the opposite sex. The shyness, vulnerability and nervousness around the opposite sex all came from past conditioning.

Paula wanted to settle down and have children, get married and become a mum, she said it's all that she ever dreamed of and came to me for some support sessions to work out how she could overcome the block she felt she had around commitment. She had a belief that by entering relationship her life would be over in some way because she would have to agree to certain things in the relationship that she might not like.

We explored Paula's past and worked through many aspects of her life experience. Paula had a very strict upbringing, her parents and grandparents were very Victorian in their attitude and did not allow Paula the personal freedom she wanted whilst growing up. Although Paula eventually left home at the age of thirty five and was living with roommates in a house share when she came to see me, she still spoke with her parents every day and saw them regularly. She shared with me that her parents would constantly quiz her about friends, what she was doing with her spare time, how she was spending her money and were very critical and judgemental of her choices in lots of ways.

Paula felt like she had to constantly report back to her parents about her every move and admitted that she was scared to have a relationship, in case her parents didn't approve of her choice in men. She confessed that she didn't think any man would want to meet her interfering parents. Paula felt that no matter how hard she tried to gain her parents' acceptance and approval of her, it was like fighting a losing battle.

Paula shared memories with me of her childhood - of being sent to her room for what seemed like hours and hours and if she tried to come back downstairs to join her parents, they would often shout at her and she would be made to stay even longer in her room in silence. Paula was often sent to her room without her evening meal, anytime she expressed her feelings as a child. She recounts feeling banished, bad, rejected and unloved she also felt very lonely, cold and afraid as well as hungry and didn't understand on many occasions why she was sent to her room. When Paula attempted to ask why she had been sent to her room, she would receive no explanation and was just told to mind her manners. Paula would cry for hours feeling that all she wanted was to be held, understood and comforted. Instead, she was left with silence, coldness and felt very alone.

Paula really felt like she was treading on egg shells around her parents, she was unsure what to say and what not to say and was in conflict between living the life she wanted for herself and also living the life her parents saw fit for her. Even at the age of thirty five, she still felt like her parents treated her as a five-year old and would carry around with her their internalised voices of judgement, criticism and disapproval.

Paula became a bit of a rebel, when she left home; she was out most of the time and only went back to her rented flat to sleep when she was exhausted. Paula was good at putting on an act in front of others; she was the life and soul of the party, which attracted many men to her. She was able to reveal the happy, cheery side of herself to potential partners, but when it came to real intimacy and communication, she was not able to open up and share her thoughts, fears, hopes or dreams. It's as though she kept herself safe, by keeping herself busy and keeping close relationships at arm's length.

Paula said sometimes she just felt like disappearing, that she wondered if she should just leave her hometown and go travelling, to get away from the unfulfilling life she felt she was living.

Insightful Questions

Take a moment to reflect on the case study that you have just read and answer the following questions. By doing so you will gain awareness around past relationships and how those relationships may be influencing your future.

As adults we often forget that it's ok to take responsibility in making decisions for ourselves. People will always have an opinion based on their own life experiences. At some point we need to stop reacting from the child part of ourselves that is trapped there in an adult body. EFT will support you in clearing any emotions that may get in your way of feeling able to act and react from the adult part of you.

- **Do you relate to Paula in any way?**

- **Do you also need the love, approval and acceptance from your parents, friends and significant others, before you will allow yourself to be in the relationships of your choice?**

- **What aspects of Paula's life and upbringing may be similar to your own?**

- **How has this affected you and your life choices?**

- **Are you really where you want to be in terms of love and relationships?**

- **Who (including yourself) might be getting in your way of having the relationships of your choice?**

- **How would your life change if you were able to let go of the past and move on?**

- **What opportunities would letting go of the past give you? What have been the negative consequences of holding onto the past and how has this affected you and your love relationships?**

Paula was able to work out where her fears came from, she didn't want a cold and argumentative relationship, like her parents have, she didn't want to be controlled and told what she could and couldn't say or do, she didn't want to be ignored or rejected, and she didn't want to feel isolated and alone in a relationship. All the things she didn't want were a reflection of different aspects of her life growing up. Because Paula's focus was on what she didn't want, she expected all her relationships to be like those of her parents.

Paula realised that she had never given anyone the chance to prove her beliefs about relationships wrong. She had never paid attention to her friends' relationships which were, in fact, very loving, happy and communicative partnerships. Paula realised that she was only focusing on all the negative aspects of a relationship, instead of all the positive things that were often present in loving and communicative relationships.

Paula used The Spotlight Process to clarify where her fear-based thinking came from, we worked together using EFT to clear those fears and gained an acceptance that her parents brought her up in the way they too had been bought up and didn't know any other way, they literally were just operating from how they had experienced their own parenting.

During our work together, Paula decided it would be good for her to speak to her parents about how she was feeling, openly and honestly. She asked to meet with her parents and she spoke with them for the first time as an adult. She asked them that they just listen, without speaking, as what she had to say was important. Having this talk with her parents, in fact, bought them together much closer as a family.

Paula's dad had tears in his eyes when she told her parents how she felt, her dad explained that he only ever wanted her to do well in life and not to hurt her and that he did love her very much, but that he had been bought up not to show his feelings. The three of them had a slightly stiff cuddle, laughing and holding back their tears. Her parents said that they realised Paula wasn't a child anymore and was entitled to a life of her own. There was such freedom in having this conversation - one that she had been avoiding for years.

Her relationship with her mum became much more balanced, as her mum revealed to Paula that growing up she, too, felt lonely and isolated and married Paula's dad because her parents approved of him and said he would be the decent type to marry.

The truth is we become so comfortable with our beliefs and our stories, that until we wake up, we aren't aware that there are alternative choices and beliefs available to us.

TELLING THE SAME OLD STORIES

After years of telling our stories and believing them as the truth, this may become all we talk and think about. We may become accustomed to think about our past with anger, blame, regret, bitterness and disappointment. Every time we revisit the negative past, we go into a cycle of negative thoughts, feelings and emotions, constantly reacting to 'old stuff' and old stories.

The only person suffering is you. The past only exists in our heads and it's us who decides what we think about, no one else.

Making gradual change in your thinking and actions, making a commitment to yourself and taking full responsibility for the rest of your life being the best of your life can only serve you and bring you closer to the love and relationships that you desire.

Power Questions

It could be that you want to change the dynamics in some of your relationships just as Paula did. Sometimes what we fear saying or doing is never as bad as what we expect it to be.

Work through the following questions

- **How would moving on from the past benefit you?**
- **How would you be thinking differently?**
- **What might you have to stop doing, start doing or do differently to improve your relationships?**
- **What opportunities might come your way if you are able to let go of the past hurts?**
- **What are you choosing for yourself right now, fear or love?**

And the day came when the risk to remain tight in a bud was more painful than the risk it took to blossom – Anais Nin

Chapter 5

The Present

THE PRESENT

IT'S TIME TO STOP SHINING YOUR LIGHT IN THE PAST BECAUSE THAT'S NOT WHERE THE FUTURE IS

From this moment on, I invite you to get into the mindset of planning ahead for a new and exciting journey to a brand new destination – your future!

As well as getting curious about all the appealing opportunities ahead, I encourage you to keep track of your thoughts and what you say inside your own mind or out loud. The words that you say to yourself or out loud in short, are more powerful than you could ever imagine. Please monitor your thoughts from here on in, speaking only of those which are supportive to you and your love and relationship goals. If you have old stories that you keep sharing and retelling, that do not have you jumping for joy, with respect, it's time to close those chapters and start a whole new book.

You can't move on with the next chapter of your life if you keep re reading the last one – author unknown

USING YOUR PAST TO WORK FOR YOU

Today is the first day of the rest of your life and it's up to you to make it a good one.

I will guide you to get clear on what you want for your future and support you to getting down to the business of shaping and creating your reality, so that you step more fully into a positive expression of yourself, to be all that you are, true to you and authentic to your heart's desires.

YOU ARE THE PILOT OF YOUR LIFE

You are in the hot seat, it's down to you now to set the destination and plan the journey, you have everything you need to charter your course and enjoy the ride.

There is so much potential and possibility ahead and with your commitment, intention and desire, I have faith in you that because you're focused on what you want, you can be, do and have all that you have dreamt of and more.

OUT WITH THE OLD AND IN WITH THE NEW

This chapter will be a journey of discovery where you leave behind old territory, old ways of thinking, old beliefs and old fears.

The journey so far may have been a roller coaster of emotions where you have acknowledged the past, gained the learning and wisdom that you may not have been aware of before and you are now ready to apply that knowledge to make the rest of your life the best of your life.

CREATING A BRIGHT NEW FUTURE

It's time to check out your suitcase and decide not to pack the things that have been weighing you down and holding you back from living the life you want and deserve.

In fact, why not treat yourself to a brand new suitcase...the best is yet to come and this is going to be one hell of a ride!

 **Heart based exercise
(20 minutes)**

MY IDEAL DAY

'My Ideal Day' is a creative way to get you thinking in a more positive and optimistic way and will move you beyond any limited thinking, to a place where all things are possible, encouraging you to live your life with passion and purpose. When you focus on what you want as if it is already yours, it is likely to show up much sooner than you think.

On a brand new sheet of paper or in your journal, write a story about a day in your life. This will be no ordinary day, it will be the story of your ideal day and how it will be if you have everything you want - think specifically here about love and relationships and include that in the main content of your writing.

- **How will you be thinking differently?**
- **What will your day look like?**
- **What will be happening?**
- **How will you be feeling?**
- **What will you hear going on around you?**
- **How will you be spending your time?**

Write this story from the truth of who you are (not someone you feel you 'have' to be), write it from your heart space where you are open to giving and receiving love.

Take time to go over your story, making sure it's complete and then read your story every day for a week.

By focusing on what you want, rather than what you don't want and getting into the energy space of having what you dream of, your dreams are more likely to become a reality. It is also very uplifting to be thinking from the place of what is possible and that everything you have included in your ideal day is achievable.

You will be writing this in the present tense, as if what you want has already come to pass and you are enjoying your life and love relationships.

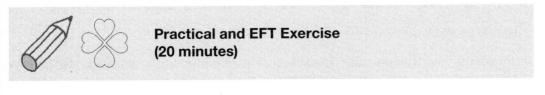

**Practical and EFT Exercise
(20 minutes)**

I have included a few ideas here to get you in the groove of acting 'as if'. You can follow these pointers adding in your own positive endings in your journal or writing your ideal day from scratch in story form.

RAISING YOUR LOVE VIBRATION

Use the following statements in addition to the written exercise as you tap through your tapping points, speaking out loud as you fill the gaps with your own examples.

I love how it feels when.....

I love knowing.....

It makes me feel so good that.....

I love seeing myself.....

I enjoy.....

I'm excited at the thought of.....

I love being.....

I'm delighted that....

I appreciate....

It feels so good to be....

I'm so happy that....

Be sure to read your story every day for a week (or longer if you wish to) and start to notice how differently you feel about yourself and your future. When you can change your mind set about what is possible rather than what is impossible this changes your energetic vibration, try it and see.

It is my wish for you that you can recognise just how far you have come already on your journey to finding you and finding love and to realise that you are far more capable of creating a life of your dreams than you ever imagined.

My wish for you is that you see your true worth, your true power, your true essence because who you are is amazing.

This book is in honour of who you are and comes from my heart to yours with love.

GET TO THE HEART OF LOVE AND RELATIONSHIPS

Wherever you go, go with all your heart - Confucius

Your heart is much more than a vessel for romance. Your heart holds the natural ability to love and is the essence of who you are.

Your heart is very wise, it knows all the answers to all your questions and if you listen to it, it will support you in acting from the core of your being.

Your heart provides you with valuable information; it is where you store joy and compassion for yourself and others. It stores that which you seek...love.

The heart is a powerful transmitter and radiates an energetic pulse. It is 5,000 times more powerful than the brains magnetic field. The Institute of HeartMath in California has carried out some fantastic research in this area of study.

A GLASS FULL OF LOVE

You, yourself have the ability to fill your glass up with self love. You have the endless capacity to love and that love begins with the relationship you have with yourself. Thinking, feeling and acting from the heart of love will bring love to you.

You may be someone who up to now has responded predominantly from your head, perhaps your heart has been hurt and you have put walls up around it to protect yourself. Perhaps you trusted someone and they let you down, so it may have felt unsafe in the past for you to open your heart to love.

Explore living and thinking from your heart. Whether dwelling in the past, present, or future, moment by moment you have control over your thoughts.

By choosing to think and respond from your heart space and notice the difference, as opposed to thinking solely from the head, you will discover how operating from your heart space has the potential to change how you see yourself, others and the world around you.

CONNECTING WITH YOUR HEART SPACE

Heart Breathing is a fantastic tool that will calm you. It can be used at the start of the EFT process or as a standalone aid which will bring you back to your centre.

This exercise is shared with kind permission of Kate Marillat and featured in Transform Your Beliefs, Transform Your Life

 Using Heart Breathing – a practical heart focused exercise (15 minutes)

1. **Sit back in a comfortable chair and close your eyes**

2. **Put either hand over your heart and focus your attention into that area, into those deep chambers in the centre of your chest**

3. **Breathe deeply but normally and feel as if your breath is coming out of your heart area**

4. **Begin to regulate your breathing to count of six**

5. **Breath in for a count of six into your heart space**

6. **Breathe out for a count of six out of your heart space**

7. **Keep breathing in for the count of six and out for the count of six**

8. **Focus on your heart area and feel the relaxation**

Heart breathing will relax and calm you. Just like using EFT if you are feeling emotionally overwhelmed, Heart Breathing can also be used in the moment.

An open heart is an open mind – Dalai Lama

 Thought power

The first step to understanding your thoughts, feelings, emotions, and behaviours, is to monitor your self-talk. Becoming aware of the constant stream of internal chatter and noticing what you say to yourself and how you say it, is the first step in awareness and from that point, you can literally catch your thoughts and change them to those which are more positive.

Spend time noticing the content of the chatter using The Spotlight Process and where it is focused (past, present or future?) This is not about criticising yourself for thinking in a self limiting way, or to berate yourself, the exercise is designed for you to be very gentle and loving with yourself.

The idea is that you go into a space of just noticing your thinking, without attaching any label to it 'good' or 'bad'. Not judging yourself as right or wrong, just noticing the content of the thought and acknowledging it in the same way you might notice clouds passing across a blue sky, just noticing them, and being aware of your thoughts and if they are coming to you from the past, present or future.

I AM NOT MY THOUGHTS

Over time and with loving kindness, you will be able to reassure yourself that you are in fact just having thoughts, whatever the content of the thought, that's all it is, just a thought that you are creating in your mind that causes an energetic response in your body. EFT can be applied to any distressing thoughts, to bring your energy back into alignment.

Gently remind yourself that your thoughts are not always fact and are often a replay of a story from the past and an old energetic response that can often easily be transformed using EFT.

Spending time thinking about your thoughts may not be something we normally do, but unless we challenge and correct the negative internal voice, it may continue to nag at us in unhelpful ways.

RECOGNISING THE EARLY WARNING SIGNS THAT YOU'RE REACTING FROM THE PAST

Your body is always your best advisor, it responds to your internal dialogue of thoughts and words, listen to it and you will learn so much about yourself and how you react to different things.

By listening to your body, you will start to notice more and more how your body reacts energetically to internal thoughts and to external events, people and situations. You will either feel low, neutral, or high energetic vibrations or somewhere in between, depending on what you are thinking about and reacting to. The idea is to become aware of how your body reflects your thoughts and feelings and using that awareness to bring balance to your thinking which will, in turn, bring balance to your emotions and overall wellbeing.

Thought is energy which is carried through the body and your body will always have a physical reaction to a thought.

As you go throughout your day, be aware of what words you use inside your own mind that brings you and your energy down.

Often, unresolved emotions will keep being re-triggered unless you do something to transform them. You can self correct an unbalanced thought and regulate any overwhelming emotions using EFT.

THINKING A BETTER THOUGHT

You can also, practically, think about 'a better thought' i.e. instead of telling yourself 'I feel really sad', you may wish to replace it with 'this sadness will soon pass' or 'this sadness is only energy and I'm ok', 'this sadness is part of my healing process and I'm working through it', as you tap through your tapping points.

Rather than becoming a victim of the past, you have the power and ability to choose how to use your past to your best advantage.

The feelings you have about yourself are so important, your thoughts are like seeds that will germinate and grow. If you think you're unlovable, not good enough, worthless etc these thoughts will grow like weeds spreading far and wide.

However, you are now equipped to work through where your beliefs came from, why they were formed and the purpose the belief may have had for you.

You will be able to transform the belief into new seeds of truth and have yourself a beautiful garden of hopes and dreams.

Planting Your Seeds of Truth

Working through this section you will gain an awareness of what emotions and memories may still need to be worked through. The more you question your thinking and regulate it using The Spotlight Process and EFT, the more benefits you will notice:

Any time you feel yourself being re-triggered and recognise the early warning signs that you are going back down the slippery slope to the past, any time you experience any sort of emotional overwhelm, you can ask yourself the following questions and repeat the statements, whilst tapping through your points and listen in carefully to what your mind and body are telling you.

THOUGHT TRACKING USING THE SPOTLIGHT PROCESS

 **Insightful Exercise
(10 minutes)**

Use this exercise 'in the moment' if you are able to or as a reflection exercise at your earliest opportunity to track your thought process.

- **What am I feeling in this moment?**
- **How does this feeling relate to my past?**
- **When was the first time I felt this way?**
- **How often between then and now have I felt this way?**
- **What belief did I form from experiencing this feeling?**
- **How has this belief affected my life?**
- **Is this belief hindering me or helping me?**
- **If I was able to let go of this belief that was formed in the past, what would that leave space for?**
- **I am willing to release this old belief of.....**
- **What new and empowering belief can I choose to transform the past?**
- **I am willing to accept my new belief that.....**
- **I choose to use my past, for my highest good**
- **I am willing to let go of the past and step into the future**

There is no evidence that the past will repeat itself again, it is purely our thinking that tells us so.

MY ADVICE IS 'DON'T BELIEVE EVERYTHING YOU THINK'. GROWING FROM THE PAST IS PRODUCTIVE, LIVING THERE ISN'T.

I'm going to list some key words that may change your energy vibration as you read them. It's possible that you have a memory of each of these emotions and feelings stored in your energetic system. It's really important for you to realise just how much your thinking will affect your physiology, your actions and behaviours, either creating balance or imbalance. The words you think create thoughts and they in turn, create emotions/feelings/changes in energy which creates results and actions in your life.

Whatever emotional reactions you experience, trace them back to the original thought or word you started off with, i.e. if you experience sadness and tell yourself 'I feel so sad', this will create emotions of sadness, apathy, a sense of loss or perhaps grief and you may take to your bed, avoid new relationships and feel that life and love are hopeless. The alternative is to gently and kindly guide yourself back to choosing different and empowering thoughts and high energy thinking, as listed on the second table.

LOW ENERGY THINKING VERSES HIGH ENERGY THINKING

 **Practical Exercise
(10 minutes)**

Copy out this list of low energy and high energy words as a reminder of low and high energy thoughts. Being aware of how often you think a low energy thought and changing it to one that is higher in energy will serve you well.

Use EFT to transform any lingering low energy emotions that are thoughts being projected into the future, or which are based on past negative experiences that you are replaying in your mind. Read through and bring your awareness to the thoughts and words that you experience to most. When you think a low energy thought your body will respond to that thought.

Low energy thinking	
Sleepy	Tired
Apathetic	Bored
Isolated	Lonely
Inferior	Depressed
Stupid	Ashamed

Remorseful	Guilty
Distant	Hurt
Sarcastic	Hostile
Frustrated	Angry
Jealous	Selfish
Irritated	Hateful
Sceptical	Critical
Bewildered	Confused
Discouraged	Rejected
Insignificant	Helpless
Inadequate	Submissive
Embarrassed	Insecure
Overwhelmed	Anxious
High energy thinking	
Relaxed	Content
Responsive	Intimate
Serene	Loving
Secure	Trusting
Thankful	Nurturing
Confident	Faithful
Valuable	Appreciated
Worthwhile	Respected
Successful	Proud
Surprised	Aware
Optimistic	Hopeful
Playful	Creative
Amused	Cheerful
Stimulating	Energetic
Fascinating	Sensuous
Daring	Excited

- **After reading through and getting a better understanding of low and high energy thinking, which do you prefer?**
- **Are you able to tell the difference physically when you alternate between low and high energy thoughts?**

Our thoughts influence our energetic vibration and being aware of this now, I feel sure that you will be more self aware in the future of when your thoughts limit you in some way.

- **What words, thoughts and feelings had your body slumping and feeling drained and de-motivated?**
- **Which words, thoughts and feelings set your heart racing with excitement and anticipation?**

We are sometimes our own worst enemies. We may be critical of ourselves, finding fault and judging ourselves negatively. We may compare ourselves to others and let the past influence the future.

The good news is it's possible to bring our thoughts into check and re address the balance of negative and positive thinking.

**Power Exercise
(apply daily as often as possible)**

For the next few days, observe how many of your thoughts are self critical and how many love. Keep a tally of these in your journal or your phone perhaps, you will be surprised I think at how many are negative.

For every critical thought you have, replace it with a thought that is kinder and more loving.

All change begins with taking action and would you agree it's time to change your thinking to that which is more loving?

THE NEEDS OF THE HEART

It is always possible to be more loving towards ourselves, once we know what our needs are. When we are able to meet those needs independently, we take control of our lives.

When we open our hearts and give love to ourselves, then and only then can we love and honour others and be open to receiving love.

When we are able to experience love from within without being dependent on another for love, we gain a new sense of strength and optimism.

LOVE IS AN INSIDE JOB

There is a lot of liberation in looking after your own needs rather than hoping some-one else will. When we put conditions and demands on others to love us, we may be let down.

When we welcome love that can be given freely and without insistence that it be given, the other person is able to give love more willingly and easily.

We may have learnt somewhere along the way that relationships are all about an-other person making us feel worthy, lovable and complete though that is in fact our own responsibility as adults to provide those things for ourselves.

If we put our self worth outside of ourselves, this often leads to the feelings of being rejected and feeling abandoned and we may become disappointed when our needs aren't met, we may become resentful and frustrated when someone isn't doing what we think they 'should' be doing to make us feel good.

Clinging to relationships because we may feel that something is missing in our lives, or because we may feel insecure in some way will further lead to the feeling that we are powerless in love. In fact, we are more powerful than we ever gave ourselves credit for.

RELATIONSHIPS AS MIRRORS OF WHO WE ARE

Relationships are a mirror of who you are and when you love yourself and improve the relationship that you have with yourself, this will be reflected back to you in the relationships that you choose for yourself.

You will not be coming from a place of need and lack, but from a place of wholeness.

INTIMACY BEGINS WITH YOU

Intimacy begins with you, when you are able to be intimate with yourself, to allow all of yourself to be all of who you are and you are able to meet your own needs. It will not matter if you are single, married, divorced or widowed, you will never lose sight of your lovability.

We do not need to look outside of ourselves for love when we have love within. When we take care of our own needs, it doesn't mean we have to stay single and abstain from relationships, it simply means that we are able to take care of our-selves within all our relationships.

ACCEPTING OTHERS AS THEY ARE

Love is about accepting the person we are in a relationship with as they are, in turn we will be accepted as we are. We are happy, regardless of how they choose to behave and we develop more trust in ourselves that we can meet our own needs.

If we do not like the way someone behaves towards us, we no longer blame ourselves and think that there is something wrong with us, we do not obsess about what we may be doing wrong or not doing, we do not think up a hundred reasons why we think they don't love us. We meet our own needs every step of the way.

We learn that other people's behaviours and actions is 'their stuff', we don't need to make it about us, or reject ourselves based on their "lack of ability" to love us in the way we might desire.

Each of us is having a relationship with ourselves as well as the relationship we have with others, both need to be balanced.

COMMUNICATING THE HEARTS NEEDS IN RELATIONSHIPS

We can communicate our needs to others as part of a loving and equal relationship, though if our needs are not met by another, we still feel empowered by speaking up and being true to ourselves.

If we are consistently honest with ourselves and others about our needs, we no longer feel disempowered. There is no hidden neediness below the surface, you voice your thoughts and feelings assertively knowing that if those needs aren't met by others you can are still loveable and whole.

OTHERS ARE NOT RESPONSIBLE FOR OUR HAPPINESS, WE ARE

I am not saying you should stay in a relationship where you are unhappy, but to realise that often how a person behaves is more about them and their own personal life experiences than it is about you.

We might get into a habit of misinterpreting another person's actions, or lack of action and creating a false picture of the relationship. This is why The Spotlight Process is so important, when we can trace back what we are reacting to (often the past), once we can transform and let go of the old behaviours and habitual ways of responding in our relationships we are able to bring in new ways of reacting and responding to others.

COMMUNICATION IS THE KEY

Communication is important. Communication is about how we communicate internally, inside our own minds, as well as how we communicate outwardly to others.

Outward communication, voicing our thoughts and needs, may leave us feeling vulnerable, though it's important to stay true to who you are within the relationship. This includes voicing your thoughts and feelings calmly and constructively.

If we are unable to be honest and real in a relationship, we are like actors pretending, behaving as we think the other person wants us to behave and we lose all sense of self.

SPEAKING OUTWARDLY WHAT WE'RE FEELING INWARDLY

When we speak up, no matter how difficult that can be at times, we may anticipate our needs not being acknowledged or fulfilled by another.

By learning to voice your thoughts and needs, it gives you strength. Voicing your thoughts becomes ok for you, you communicate in a way that states your wholeness, not your neediness.

Many of us automatically assume our relationships will meet all our needs; this is seldom discussed at any stage in the relationship and is only communicated when something doesn't go our way.

Based on our expectations of the other person and what we hope for in a relationship, we expect them to mind read, to be there at the drop of a hat, to be everything to us that we cannot be to ourselves and then communication (or lack of it) leads to arguments, disagreements and major blow outs.

IF YOU WANT YOUR RELATIONSHIPS TO CHANGE, START WITH YOURSELF FIRST

Relationships are based on how we relate to ourselves first and foremost. It is never too late to start communicating clearly, to request what you would like the other person to provide for you and what having that need met would mean to you and likewise the person you are relating with can also make requests of you.

Relationships require clear communication and once you know what your needs are and you have the ability to clearly communicate them (long before chucking things across the room at each other starts) you are more likely to have a happy and harmonious relationship!

If, the person you are asking to meet one of your needs cannot do this for whatever reason, you will not abandon or reject yourself as unworthy or unlovable, you will become more open to exploring the meanings behind someone not agreeing to your request. There may be times when your nearest and dearest asks things of you that you cannot or don't want to do, but that doesn't necessarily mean that you love them any less. Each of us as adults is responsible for ourselves, we are responsible for our thoughts, our feelings and how we react to people and events.

When you take care of yourself and act in kind and loving ways towards yourself you will open the door to others to be caring and loving towards you.

AWAKENING THE HEART

Follow your heart, but be quiet for a while first. Ask questions then feel the answer. Learn to trust your heart – Anon

THE HEART QUADRANT - WHAT DOES MY HEART NEED?

**Creative Heart Based Exercise
(20 minutes)**

Ask yourself "what does my heart need right now?" and see how it answers.

Being aware of your own needs and how you can meet them for yourself is a huge turning point in improving your love relationships. Also, consider your unmet needs from childhood; it is never too late to meet those needs now as an adult.

Sometimes, we lose connection with our hearts. We go into our heads looking outside of our hearts for love, instead of looking within.

Copy out the picture of heart quadrant in your journal or on pieces of paper.

Write inside your heart shaped flower petals, what your heart does in fact need. You may have never even stopped to think about what your heart needs, but it knows the best way for you to show it love.

Write inside as many of these heart shaped flowers as you can, all the choices, affirmations, loving statements and acknowledgements that make you feel loving and lovable.

Completing this exercise daily on waking and sleeping as well as throughout the day if you are able to will have a dramatic effect on your self-worth, confidence and lovability. Honouring, respecting and loving yourself is an inside job.

I know that having come this far, you are aware that taking responsibility to look after yourself, to provide for yourself what your heart needs, the future will be so different for you now, a future full of hope, possibility, optimism and joy.

We are not held back by the love we didn't receive in the past, but by the love we are not extending in the present – Marianne Williamson

MY HEART SAYS YES AND MY HEAD SAYS NO

Head and heart can be in conflict at different times, two parts of you in disagreement, battling with each other for pole position. Have you found yourself unable to make decisions based on that inner conflict, not knowing which way to go?

A question I would like you to become familiar with is:

'AM I IN MY HEAD OR AM I IN MY HEART?'

Often times we are so much in our heads and so far removed from love, that we wouldn't recognise it if it came up and stared us in the face.

Our heads analyse and we are constantly weighing up the pros and cons of a situation. It's where our voice of doom lives and rears its ugly head until we rein it in. Our head is where fear resides and comes up with all the reasons why anything outside of our comfort zone is too risky, dangerous and should be avoided. If we're not careful, we could let our heads rule our hearts and our future, never considering the heart's needs or wants.

OPENING YOUR HEART

An open heart is very powerful, it has the capacity to love and be loved.

- **Your heart is wise.**
- **If you listen to it you will find that it knows all the answers to all your questions.**
- **Your heart provides you with valuable sources of information.**
- **Your heart has a blueprint for happiness, joy and compassion for yourself and others.**
- **Your heart stores that which you seek...love**

The heart is where our true self resides, that place of inner knowing and intuition, the higher self, the source, our oneness.

Our heart speaks to us in a gentle voice and will guide us back home to ourselves if we stop and listen.

Our heart truly knows what's best for us if we can get the head out of the way.

FOLLOWING YOUR HEART IS THE PATH TO LOVE

Now is the perfect time to love, when we let go of the past and move forward into the unknown, we grow magnificently and step fully into our power. From this moment on, think love, talk of love, act with love, eat, drink and sleep love. Make love your ultimate goal.

 Heart Based Exercise (15 minutes)

- **Listen to your heart's needs**
- **Be aware of the fears in your head**
- **Make a note of where these fears come from using The Spotlight Process. Are they fears from the past, fears related to current concerns or fears about things you imagine happening in the future?**
- **Transform and release fear using EFT**
- **Bring yourself back to your heart each time you find yourself going back into your head**
- **Go back to the heart space using heart based breathing, connect with and expand that feeling of love**
- **Act from the heart in every situation**

Heart Based Exercise
(apply this exercises for as long as it takes to bring your thoughts and heart back to balance)

In addition to the above exercise, wear a loose elastic band, hair tie, charity wrist band or just your watch around your wrist. Every time you go into your head (over analysing, judging, labelling and categorising) which takes you further away from love, change the item over from one wrist to the other, to bring you back to heart centred awareness.

Filter your experiences through your heart space and you will experience life through the filter of love.

It's a very effective and simple exercise that further brings awareness to your thought process and will aid you to re-direct your thinking to that which is more positive. It will show you the habits of your thinking and make you realise where your mind wanders to...you just need to pull it back again.

I offer this exercise to my clients and some of the feedback I've had is '' I can't believe how many of my thoughts are negative and critical '', ''Although I got annoyed at how many times I had to change the band over, it made me laugh when I realised half of what I was worrying about might not even happen''. ''My wife and I are now doing this together, I want my dad to do it too and he is so negative'' (of course this in itself is a negative thought and the band has to be changed over to the opposite wrist)

Have fun along the way catching yourself, the more you practice the more you get your thinking under control.

May your choices reflect your hopes not your fears – Nelson Mandela

COMMUNICATION

HOW ARE YOU RELATING?

How you relate right now in your life, will be the direct result of what you have learnt about love and relationships from birth to now.

Your experience of how you have been related to in the past and the meanings and perceptions you have placed on previous relationships will be filtering into this present time.

Relating is all about communicating and includes how we relate to others and how we relate to ourselves.

**Insightful Exercise
(5 minutes)**

Think of a negative and upsetting conversation from a current or previous relationship. Consider how you were relating (communicating) by answering the questions below

- **Who were you relating to?**
- **What were you relating?**
- **Why were you relating?**
- **How were you relating?**
- **Where were you relating?**
- **When were you relating?**
- **What happened when you were relating?**

As well as tone and pitch of voice, relating also includes our various communication styles, our body language and the content of what we say and how we say it.

Sometimes we think we are communicating well though at other times what we want to say and what we say are two very different things.

Take a look and explore the various communication styles here and see which communication styles you tend to adopt.

Use the information to bring your relating back into balance, if you feel that there is any room for improvement.

ASSERTIVE: Standing at an appropriate distance from another with an upright, still, relaxed and open body posture with eye to eye contact. Communication is direct, positive, responsible, honest and accepting.

PASSIVE: Weak body language, avoiding eye contact, fiddling with clothes or hair, quiet tone of voice, apologetic, moaning, helpless communication style.

INDIRECT AGGRESSION: Rolling eyes, mean looks, looking away from the other person, physically turning away from them. Communication style is controlling, sly, deceiving and manipulative.

DIRECT AGGRESSION: Challenging eye contact, hands on hips, invades personal space moving body too close to another's, wringing of hands. Communication style is bossy, impatient and overbearing.

PUTTING THE RELATE BACK INTO RELATIONSHIPS

Once we are aware of our relating style we can make changes to that style of communicating, if it is not effective in either having a loving relationship with ourselves or with others. We can learn to master different and more effective relating styles.

Case Study – Tanya

Tanya sought my support in her mid thirties, following many failed relationships. She had become pregnant at the age of fifteen and in all honesty wasn't coping well with being a mother, trying to find work as well as childcare and managing the whirlwind of emotions she experienced daily. Tanya had moved to and from different family members' homes with her daughter, but still didn't have the feeling of anywhere being home, or have the ability and confidence to parent her daughter in the way she wanted.

When she lived with her mother, she was also exposed to the bouts of bad tempers, arguments and fights between her mother and step father, both of whom were often drunk and would involve her in their arguments.

Tanya had many occasions of living with her grandmother and whilst living there, experienced great sadness, as her grandmother would be high and happy one moment and the next, take to her bed for weeks on end, grumbling and swearing at Tanya and her daughter. Tanya felt responsible for her grandmother's wellbeing as well as her daughters and felt she couldn't leave her daughter in her grandmother's care while she looked for work. She felt trapped with a sense of hopelessness about the future.

Tanya's ex partner appeared back in her life, whilst we were working together. There would be times when he would see his daughter, but he was also very unreliable. Also, Tanya found herself falling back into his arms each time he came to see their daughter. Part of her enjoyed the connection the other part of her heated herself or starting up where the relationship left off, only for him to leave all over again with no idea when he was coming back.

I worked with Tanya using The Spotlight Process and we discussed and explored her past relationships. The theme running throughout, was angry communication styles from parents, grandparents and partners and in school, she had experienced many unhappy times trying to fit in, she had been expelled numerous times and had gained a reputation as a trouble maker, as she was not able to express her emotions constructively and clearly, she would often explode when her frustration and anger built up to boiling point.

Tanya had not seen her father since the age of six and wondered what was wrong with her for him to disappear from her life. She chose male partners and lovers, who were never truly available and would not commit to a lasting relationship, in many ways they reflected the behaviour of her father and stepfather (angry, unreliable, verbally abusive and distant).

Tanya made great progress, once she realised that she had been learning from her parents all along about communicating in ways that weren't helpful for her. She understood how the way she responded to others made the situation worse. After some soul searching and working with Tanya to find the way back to herself and to help her realise and appreciate that she was beautiful, lovable and worthy, despite how others behaved around her, for the first time she started to believe that not all future relationships would be hostile, angry and cause heartache.

Tanya made great progress in our time together; her communication style became more assertive and she became able to express her needs succinctly to her family and the father of her child. She moved home and rented a flat of her own to care for her daughter and also enrolled in various college courses to support her career aspirations. Tanya found childcare from reliable friends with children and the mums took it in turns to look after each other's youngsters, while the other mums worked, studied or ran day to day errands.

Tanya decided to remain single and take her time to fully resolve her relationship issues using The Spotlight Process and EFT and in doing so, improved the relationship that she had with herself tenfold. She became self assured, confident and most of all realised that regardless of her past, she is a wonderful young woman who has a lot to offer a potential partner.

By staying single while she worked through the process of finding herself, she found love, ultimately from herself first and foremost. Tanya knew that she would recognise straight away if any potential suitor was not going to be a supportive and loving partner for her and is very clear about what she wants for the future. She turned her 'don't wants' to 'do wants' and her dreams into plans.

This is just one of the reasons why I love the work that I do. Assisting others in finding themselves, improving the relationship that they have with themselves and learning to love and live again, is worth its weight in gold.

I feel very privileged to work with these amazing people who come to me and share their honesty and down to the bone feelings and emotions. It's from this place of being vulnerable and honest with ourselves, that the greatest progress can be made.

Be aware of which communication category you fall into and how (depending on who you are with) your style changes and how you relate differently to someone depending on their own style of communicating.

WHAT YOU THINK MIGHT BE BEING SAID AND WHAT IS ACTUALLY BEING SAID MAY BE TWO DIFFERENT THINGS

Think before you react and examine your perception of what you think is being said, rather than what you think might be being said. Sometimes we can get things totally wrong or as mentioned before, we are reacting from the past when we felt similar emotions to ones we experience in a current moment.

We may receive information from the person speaking or say things from the wounded child within, rather than the adult part of ourselves.

Be aware at all times of your own inner dialogue and how you speak to yourself about yourself or others, your relating style is important if you wish to build, transform and create loving relationships.

What you say internally may be based on old perceptions and old beliefs. Again, use The Spotlight Process to work out where these thoughts come from (past, present or future).

If there are any negative thoughts, beliefs, feelings and emotions that leave you feeling overwhelmed, use EFT to transform the emotions and to shift and change your energy. You will notice if this is working as your body will respond accordingly either feeling stressed or at ease.

Stay aware of your body language and how your body also relates your thoughts and feelings. When you want to come across as assertive, calm and in control, look people gently in the eye, use hand movements that are soft and flowing to express soft and flowing emotions. Use a level voice tone and consider your choice of words before speaking.

LONELINESS AND WAKING UP FROM THE FAIRY TALE

Being single doesn't mean you're broken, damaged or undesirable - far from it.

If you have been lonely in a relationship because your significant other hasn't been physically or emotionally available this doesn't mean that you are unlovable or undeserving of their time or attention, how they respond to you is about them and not about you.

If you keep attracting the relationships that don't serve you, it's possible to change the direction of your future using The Spotlight Process and EFT, to clear old patterns of behaviour, outdated beliefs and any negative emotions that have been burning away inside you.

It's through awareness about what isn't working in your life, what is working and what you may be able to do differently in the future of your love relationships, that brings the greatest transformation.

The relationship you have with yourself and your perception of loneliness can be gently tweaked so that being by yourself is something that you enjoy and look forward to.

Case Study

Case Study – Alison

Alison thought there was something wrong with her when she came to see me as she seemed incapable of being on her own and needed to be in a relationship. From the age of sixteen, Alison had gone from one relationship to another, without any time gap in between and often had the next suitor lined up even before she finished her current relationship.

As soon as a relationship started going pear shaped as she called it and Alison's needs weren't met by her partner, she would become distant, cold and unloving in the relationship. She would withdraw her love, attention and communication and go into herself, a place where she admitted she felt lonely and isolated. She was not able to address her fears, anxieties and worries with partners. If her partner wanted a night out with friends, a weekend away on his own with family or friends, or came home late from work, for Alison, it was as though the world was going to end. She said it was as though she could feel the walls falling down around her and her world caving in.

Alison's symptoms when her partners were away from her, apart from scheduled work times, would be fear, panic, anxiety, cold sweats, tears, heart racing, headaches, wanting to sleep alternating with frantic cleaning and sorting, calling friends and family talking hysterically about her thoughts that the relationship was over, At times, Alison drank to excess to try and blot out her feelings, would call and text her partners obsessively to find out where they were and also confessed at times that she felt it would be easier not to be here. She was stressed, not sleeping well, not eating well and not taking care of herself.

Using The Spotlight Process, helped Alison identify the first time in her life where she had felt this way. We were able to trace the feeling back to the day she found out her dad had left her mum and that she had to make a decision about who to live with. This was her earliest memory of loving someone who was leaving her. We explored 'being left' and although she knew that her dad had stopped loving her mum and why he was leaving, she felt that it was her fault and that he was leaving her. She remembers sitting in her room alone feeling the exact same feelings that she didn't know when she would see her dad again. We explored the feelings of separation, loss, grief, not having control, fear and the overwhelming anxiety she felt about her future. Her family unit had been torn apart and she felt like her heart had been too.

Alison realised that as an adult she had never truly worked through the feelings of her dad leaving. Although her partners weren't leaving in the same way and were either stuck in traffic, working late, or with friends or family, Alison felt the same separation anxiety she felt as a child and the loneliness, anxiety and despair that she had experienced on that day.

Alison realised that she was confusing the current moment with the past and also projecting into the future that her partner being out automatically meant that she was about to be rejected. She realised, through our work together, that this wasn't true, but merely the little girl inside her, still reacting from the hurt part of herself. She understood how she was jumping back into the past and all of the emotions that she had experienced in that moment of shock and freezing those emotions inside herself. These feelings were re-triggered over and over every time a partner was not physically or emotionally available to her.

It was quite a revelation for Alison, she cried tears of relief when she understood as an adult what she had been doing, it's like a thousand light bulbs lit up, and she felt a sense of relief and certainly wanted to be free from self destructive thinking and behaviours.

Alison was very willing to use EFT both in her sessions and also in-between, to clear the pain from the past and transform her future. Together, we converted the whole range of emotions that Alison felt that day to those which were more positive. We were able to work with the younger part of Alison and transform the belief that she wasn't lovable, into the fact that her dad did love her very much.

Alison realised that for many years she had held onto blame, anger, resentment and fear related to her father and that in some ways she had been venting those feelings in her relationships.

Alison is now single and has been, for a couple of years, since we completed working together. Instead, she has been busy building a loving relationship with herself and a career that is meaningful and rewarding. She enjoys time out with friends, has joined new social groups and down time at home reading, gardening and listening to music and never feels alone. She is happy and content and is open in the future to having a loving relationship, though for the time being, she has stated that she has never felt happier and so in love with life.

FROM LONELINESS TO LOVE HAS SO GOT TO BE WORTH IT!

If you, too, have been experiencing loneliness, emptiness or fear of being alone then use The Spotlight Process and EFT to trace back to where you formed your beliefs about loneliness, emptiness and being alone. Then use EFT to change how you relate to yourself about this.

Being In Love – OSHO

The capacity to be alone is the capacity to love. It may look paradoxical to you, but it is not. It is an existential truth; only those people capable of being alone are capable of love, of sharing, of going into the deepest core of another person without possessing the other, without becoming dependent on the other, without reducing the other to a thing, and without being addicted to the other. They allow the other absolute freedom because they know that if the other leaves, they will be as happy as they are now. Their happiness cannot be taken by the other, because it was not given by the other.

FIND YOU, FIND LOVE

I'm sure by now, whatever point in your life you have reached you have had all kinds of relationships some that have left a happy imprint in your heart and others hurtful.

The biggest lesson I wish to share with you, is that 'all past relationships are in fact a success' as they have helped you to grow into the person you are right now. Had I not had my own relationship challenges, disappointments and heartbreaks along the way, I know for sure I would not be doing the work I love and Find YOU, Find LOVE would never have been written and so I, for one, would not change my past relationships for anything as they have led me to doing the work that I love.

STOP AND REFLECT FOR A MOMENT AND CONSIDER HOW YOUR PAST RELATIONSHIPS MAY HAVE BENEFITTED YOU

Our relationships teach us about ourselves and when you are able to explore the learning, wisdom and knowledge you have gained through having that relationship, what may once have seemed to be unbearable, may in fact have been a gift in developing you as the wonderful human being that you are.

GETTING OUT OF YOUR OWN WAY

It's very hard on the people we are in relationships with, if they do genuinely love us, want to be with us and are faithful to us, if we don't believe their actions, behaviours, words, or appreciate their presence in our lives.

I, for one, have been guilty of not realising how much I was loved, until after I had run away yet again from different relationships. In hindsight, it's this pattern of running away that kept me safe from my imagined fears but also kept me away from what I yearned for most – love. Do you recognise this pattern in yourself?

Without self love and taking personal responsibility to fulfil our own needs, we operate from a place of lack and neediness; we cannot love another or receive love until we believe ourselves to be completely whole. Unless we truly love ourselves, we will never believe someone else does.

By loving and caring for ourselves we show others that it's ok for them to love and care for us too. We are often treated by others as we treat ourselves and if we cannot love ourselves, we make it very difficult for others to love us.

Even though we may say that we want the relationship of our dreams, we might also believe that it's impossible to have a fulfilling and loving relationship. What we do want and what we don't want seem to be in conflict. Part of us may believe that true love and happiness is possible and the other part denying any thought of entertaining it. We might push love and the opportunity for true happiness away, without realising we are sabotaging ourselves.

Personal transformation occurs, once we are able to identify how we get in our own way, so we can then release and remove those inner obstacles to love.

HOW WE EXPERIENCE THINGS AND HOW THEY REALLY ARE

There is a term used in NLP, that 'the map is not the territory' which basically means whatever your experiences of love and relationships up to now, there is always a different journey ahead waiting for you - one that is totally different to the map that you have.

The map or the blueprint that you may have been holding onto, will be made up of your past love and relationship experiences and may not be the best guide to your future. It would be like covering old rocky ground and your internal Sat Nav telling you to 'turn around where possible'

It's time to tear up the map of what hasn't worked, forget about the wrong paths you may have gone down, and the dead ends you met because there is a whole new territory waiting out there for you. It's time to plan the journey based on a new destination, creating a travel plan of places you'd like to visit along the way to the journey's end. There is no point in using your old map.

THE PAST IS OVER AND YOU HAVE YOUR WHOLE LIFE AHEAD OF YOU

 **Heart Based Exercise
(10 minutes)**

I encourage you to reflect on the following points, to make your future the best it can be. Ask yourself-

- **What do I need to stop doing that hold me back from having more self love?**
- **What do I need to start doing to be open to receiving love?**
- **What do I need to do differently to improve my relationships?**
- **What can I commit to right now that will move me forwards in the direction of my dreams?**

Be aware of the thoughts, actions and behaviours which will take you closer to your dreams and then go get 'em!

Chapter 6

Looking to the Future

MOVING FORWARD IN THE DIRECTION OF YOUR DREAMS

This chapter will support you to reflect on just how far you have come already on this amazing journey to finding you and finding love, it will offer you further signposts to support you to achieve the love and relationship goals that are personal to you.

I'm so proud of you that you have worked through the preceding chapters that are the building blocks of strength and resilience for your journey ahead.

DOING THE INNER WORK

There is so much that you can achieve when you focus on the 'inner work first', instead of looking outside and expecting existing relationships to change.

CHANGE BEGINS WITHIN FIRST AND FOREMOST

Instead of waiting for love to come to you as if by a miracle, you may wish to take action in finding love. I for one did not wait for love to find me; I took action and let friends know that I was single and looking to meet a long term life partner. I attended different events in different areas. I joined several dating sites and became clearer on the type of person I was hoping to meet. It was a learning curve with some funny stories along the way and every no was one step closer to a yes.

Many of my clients have gone on to make these positive changes for themselves and although it means getting outside of your comfort zone, it will be worth the learning and personal growth opportunities that come your way.

Many of our relationships go wrong because we are living in the past, or have negative thoughts about the future of our relationships.

STAYING PRESENT

If we were able to live in the moment and react to what is happening, rather than what we think is happening, or what we are projecting, we will have more relationship success.

Using EFT and The Spotlight Process, will not only change your energy vibration; it will also change how you think about relationships, love and life in general.

When you feel good about yourself, when you understand and know deep in the heart of you that who you are is lovable, you no longer think in terms of lack, you are already full of love and this is what you will attract ...even more love!

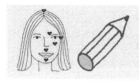 **EFT and Practical Exercise (20 minutes)**

HERE ARE MY TOP TIPS FOR PAVING THE WAY TO LOVE

Apply EFT tapping through your points, speaking the statements below out loud or inside your own mind.

For added benefit write the statements out in your journal.

- **I am ready to move on from the past using The Spotlight Process and EFT**
- **I take full responsibility for what I want in life and I am prepared to take action to get it**
- **I act as if success is already mine**
- **I make the right choices for me and I remember that I can keep changing my choices as and when I wish**
- **I trust my intuition and let it be my guide**
- **I am willing to take action and risks to achieve what I want**
- **I have a positive attitude about myself and life in general**
- **I take the initiative and use my assertiveness to make sure I achieve my goals**
- **I act from a place of truth and integrity**
- **I say yes to me**
- **I commit to taking action to transform my love relationships**

 Audio Download - Standing in the spotlight of love

This recording is available on the resources section of my website www.wendyfry.com Additional love and relationship downloads will be added to this page so please keep checking for the recordings that you feel will be supportive to you.

Imagine right now that you are directing your spotlight to all that is possible for you, allowing the rays from that light to expand ever outward.

Really feel what it feels like to experience the warmth and glow of love, make that picture bright and sharp and clear.

Turn up the sounds, smell the heady scent of love, taste the sweetness of being open to giving and receiving love.

This light is YOUR LIGHT, the guiding light bringing you back home to you, the place where love resides.

It's time to re-direct your focus to Find YOU and Find LOVE. It's not until we improve the relationship that we have with ourselves and discover how to love ourselves that we are in a position to be open to receiving love. Now is the time to visualise your future exactly as you want it to be. So much is possible for you and then some.

In the right light, at the right time, everything is extraordinary – Aaron Rose

THE SECRET OF FINDING YOU

Life, as you know up to now will have been a rollercoaster of emotions, highs and lows, good times and bad.

Have you ever noticed that just when you think you have a handle on things and life calms down, something comes up when you least expect it.

YOU ARE WHAT YOU'VE BEEN LOOKING FOR ALL ALONG

The secret of finding you in amongst the inevitable challenges life throws at us is to always remember the essence of who you are. You are amazing! You have everything inside of you that you will ever need. Instead of looking outside of yourself for love and happiness, you will begin to realise that this has been inside of you all along.

WHO YOU ARE IS LOVABLE

Love has always been a part of you and with this insight you never stray from that place of knowing that the love within you is always there as a constant, no one takes your love away, you are always whole, complete and lovable.

I believe in you and I trust that you will remind yourself that whatever happens in life from here on in, you can handle it.

Whatever love and relationship challenges come your way you will be able to navigate a path through those unchartered waters, you will ride the waves, take shelter in the storms and keep going, knowing that there is sunshine behind every cloud and still waters at the journey's end.

You will have a sense of inner knowledge that whatever your challenges they will not unhinge you and that they will, in fact, make you even stronger and more determined to achieve what you want for the future.

You realise now with new found certainty, that your setbacks will not keep you stuck but enable you to discover new ways of responding, new ways of evaluating things and you will find within you that inner strength and resilience that has got you this far will continue to get you through anything.

SPOTLIGHT ON THE FUTURE AND ALL THAT IS POSSIBLE

Shine your light on the things you want, focus on the things that lift you up, the things that bring you joy. Focus on what you love. You have ultimate control over your thoughts, guide them gently and get really clear about where you are heading, adjust your sails and let the light of your own faith in yourself never waiver, remember that you have everything inside you to weather any storm.

Take the first step in faith. You don't have to see the whole staircase. Just take the first step - Martin Luther King Jr

LOVING YOURSELF FOR THE REST OF YOUR LIFE

Heart Based Exercise
(apply daily as many of these self care choices as you can)

I have listed below some activities that will aid you in being more loving to yourself and making time for you to be with you. What can you choose from these examples that will make you feel pampered, cherished and loved and what other ways can you find to love you?

Affirmations - starting and ending the day with positive affirmations or Positive EFT statements and tapping around through your tapping points, in addition to speaking the affirmations out loud or inside your head aid towards general wellbeing creating balance and positive energy flow.

Being out in nature - connecting to nature is very healing and cleansing, being out in fresh air and green spaces restores one's emotional health and physical wellbeing on many different levels.

Boundaries - setting boundaries with others and saying 'no' to them to say 'yes' to yourself can be quite liberating. Saying no doesn't mean that you are being rude or inconsiderate; it simply means that you care about yourself enough to look after your own needs, as well as supporting others to fulfil theirs.

It may take some time and practice to say no when you mean no though in doing so, gradually, it will become easier. Many of us learn in childhood that it's not OK to put our needs first, but as adults, self care is an important part of loving yourself. When you look after your own health and wellbeing, it enables you to be in a better space to offer love and care to others and brings balance and harmony.

Complementary therapies - there are some wonderful therapies that may make you feel relaxed and at peace with yourself - for example massage, Reiki and Reflexology, as well as EFT, all are treatments which aid in the release of built up emotions in the emotional and physical body. Please check out the range of therapies that I provide on the 'about the author' page.

Eating well - choosing healthy foods that you enjoy and which are natural and energising are an important part of looking after you. Prepare for yourself delicious meals and treats with love and care. Use beautiful china to eat and drink from. Make eating a beautiful ritual where you honour your body and your health.

EFT - EFT used daily is something I encourage, as this will always support you to manage your emotions and regulate energy flow.

Exercise - Any form of exercise, whether it's walking, cycling, swimming, aerobics, dancing or using a trampoline will release endorphins (the 'happy' hormone) into your body. Exercise can make you feel energised, positive and confident and is also great for toning and shaping. Be sure to have some form of exercise in your daily routine and to build up gradually listening to your body at all times.

Rest and relaxation - down time such as listening to music, reading, taking a nap or making sure you have plenty of sleep when you need it, is a very loving way to look after yourself. You may also find meditation helps you to relax after a busy day or, as part of a daily morning ritual. Check out www.tranquility-music.co.uk Five Minute Meditations by Caroline Maidment which I highly recommend.

Self care - such as taking luxurious baths with scented oils, candles burning and using wonderful body moisturisers and having a pamper, generally all helps one's body to feel loved and cared for. Choosing carefully the outfit you will wear for the day ahead, how you style your hair and if you wear make-up, taking care to apply and wear the colours that love you are all an important part of you showing yourself love, attention and care.

When you are kind and loving towards yourself and you accept yourself exactly as you are, you have the capacity to transform, dissolve and neutralise outdated emotions about yourself and your lovability.

When you choose to act from a place of self love, it's possible to expand, connect, amplify, magnetise and bring balance to your life. Your thought processes change and you may find yourself being more positive about life in general, as well as being more positive about love.

When you are more loving towards yourself without needing to receive love and approval from another, you can give from a place of love and trust, a place of self acceptance and acknowledgement. You offer love without the need for external appreciation, validation, praise or acknowledgement, because you already appreciate and value yourself. You offer love to others without conditions and enjoy giving love without any attachment to what you hope will be returned to you.

"I vow to fiercely love you in all your forms, now and forever. I promise to never forget that this is a once in a lifetime love. And to always know in the deepest part of my soul that no matter what challenges might carry us apart, we will always find our way back to each other" - The Vow – Stuart Sendor

Can you imagine how your life would change if you made this vow to yourself today and all your days that follow?

If, every day, between waking and sleeping you said this to yourself, what do you think you would notice?

How will you be thinking differently?

How will you be feeling?

What will happen in your relationships with others when you give this unconditional love to yourself?

Accepting yourself, warts and all and acting in kind and loving ways to yourself first and foremost, will add to your pot of love. Each and every day that you repeat this vow to yourself, your pot of love will fill to overflowing. You have all the love inside of you that you will ever want and more.

Start with the vow today and tomorrow and the next day and just notice what changes within and around you.

Heart Based Practical Exercise
(20 minutes)

To track your progress in the self love department, read through the statements below and record those relevant to you.

Do you agree with each of these statements one hundred percent?

If there is any hesitation or doubt related to any of the statements, use The Spotlight Process and EFT until these statements are true for you, you will be very glad you did.

Measure the percentage of what is true for you (0-100% true)	VoC
I can satisfy my own needs	
I have self respect	
I am willing to work towards gaining more self love, self acceptance and self fulfilment	
I am secure in myself outside of a relationship	
I do not need a relationship to make me feel happy	
I take responsibility to fulfil my own needs in and out of relationships	
I feel good about myself when I'm alone	
I can solve my own problems	
I give love freely and willingly without any expectation in return	
I do not feel threatened by others when I'm in a love relationship	
I can affirm myself, I do not need others to appreciate and affirm me	
An unknown future does not frighten me	
Having a relationship is not the core of my personal identity	
I am self sufficient	
I am complete outside of a relationship	
I accept myself entirely	
I love myself unconditionally	
I love from the fullness of my heart rather than from my emptiness and neediness	
I can survive without the love of another person	
Love emerges within me from my own self esteem	
I am happy and content by myself	

I can regulate my own feelings and emotions	
I am open to and welcome love and loving relationships	
I know intuitively when a relationship is right for me	
I am confident in myself and will remain so in any relationship I may have	
I am fulfilled outside of a relationship	
I have a clear idea about my love and relationship goals	
I share my love and relationship goals with my significant other	
I take responsibility for my future love and relationship choices	
I approve of and accept myself as who I am and I am comfortable in revealing who I am	
I am able to meet my own needs outside of a relationship	
I am worthy of love	

Wherever you are no matter what the weather, always bring your own sunshine – Anthony J D'Anjelo

WHO'S IN THE DRIVING SEAT OF YOUR LIFE?

When we are born into the world, our journey is decided for us by our caretakers. In the early years of our life, our own choices may be limited and often our decisions and plans are based on those around us. As we grow older, we forget that we can take responsibility for ourselves and can make decisions based on our own needs and values.

I'D LIKE YOU TO CONSIDER, FOR A MOMENT, YOUR LIFE AS A JOURNEY.....

Imagine yourself travelling that journey by car. To make that journey you would need to decide on a destination. Without a clear idea of where you want to be, you could end up anywhere, going round in circles.

You may need a few things on your journey to make it a success:

- Fuel for energy in your car
- A map so that you can plan your route
- Water if you get thirsty or if the car overheats
- Some music for entertainment
- Some fresh fruit and snacks for sustenance
- A breakdown service card just in case you experience problems along the way

Consider what necessary things are needed on your own personal journey to get to where you want to be in terms of love and relationships:

ENTHUSIASM, HOPE, TRUST, CONFIDENCE, OPTIMISM, RESILIENCE, COURAGE, STRENGTH AND A GO GET ATTITUDE!

If you come across a red light whilst travelling, do you take the time to reflect on how far you've already travelled and how much you've achieved, or do you see it as a stop sign? Suspended in time, frozen, and cocooned inside your car and mind, seeing red!!

If you come to a cross roads, what will you do then?

Decisions, decisions, which way now? I hear you ask yourself. What if I take the wrong turning?

Hey....what if it's the right way....who thought of that?

Often we have no way of knowing which road will be the right road. We have to take a risk, a chance and muster up our self belief, telling ourselves that we will get to where we want to be, if we keep the destination in mind all the time. It's natural to get lost or go off track from time to time. The important thing here is to stop and re-focus on where we are heading and the right roads will always present themselves.

The good thing about being at a cross roads is that there is always a choice about which direction to turn. If we take a wrong turn, we simply try again. Like listening to your car's Sat Nav, you also turn around where possible.

Where is your journey taking you? Are you still held back in the past, too scared to move ahead, or are you here in the present moment considering your options.

- **So who's in the driving seat of your life?**
- **Are you driving consciously or falling asleep at the wheel?**

The past has no power over the present moment - Eckhart Tolle

TURN UP YOUR LOVE DIAL AND GET INTO THE ZONE OF LOVE

Heart Based Exercise
(apply daily as many of these self care choices as you can)

It's true, everybody's looking for love. Since we were mere babies, to be loved is a natural human need from our earliest years. As adults, we no longer have to find love from the outside; we can meet our own needs fairly and squarely.

Think about a dial with **-10** being the lowest love score, **0** being neutral and **+10** being at its highest rate of love

- **How high is your love dial right now?**

- **If your dial is anything less than a + 10 what do you need to start doing, stop doing or do differently to get it to a +10?**

- **How will your life change when you are thinking and acting from a +10?**

- **What three things do you love about yourself? (keep adding to that list so that you have a growing list of things to love and appreciate about yourself)**

- **What memories do you have of giving and receiving love?**

- **Remember how giving and receiving love felt, what you saw, heard and experienced, how was this achieved?**

- **How can you be more loving towards yourself?**

- **What would happen if you accepted, allowed and embraced more love into your life?**

- **How would your day change if you filtered for and looked for all the loving experiences you could find? When you think of all the possibilities that being more open to love could bring to you do take time to enjoy thinking about or recording those things.**

- **How would your life change if you said yes to love for now and for always?**

Reflect on your answers and if you feel you need to go back and use EFT or The Spotlight Process on any thoughts, feelings and emotions that may have triggered you, by going back and repeating the transformation process using these techniques, it will have a far greater effect in your life.

LOVE COMES IN MANY FORMS – HOW DO YOU EXPERIENCE LOVE?

Have you ever put love outside of yourself as if it's a thing that can fill up a void, a hole, a need? I know I have, that is until I learnt that love is something that we can generate within ourselves. Each of us has inside of ourselves, everything we could ever need and more.

There are so many ways to experience love. One way of experiencing love is to be in the moment. In love with loving where you're at, able to enjoy the feeling of love flowing through you with ease, neither being caught up with thinking about the past, or worrying about the future, simply accepting the present moment just as it is.

THERE ARE SO MANY WAYS TO LOVE

- Self love
- Love of another
- Love of family
- Love of a pet
- Love of your work/vocation
- Love of nature/gardening
- Love of knowledge
- Love of music
- Love of people
- Love of a faith/religion
- Love of a hobby
- Love of exercise
- Love of reading/writing/journaling
- Love of stillness/meditation

What other ways can you think of that create the 'flow' in you (flow is the feeling of wholeness, connection, contentment, just being in love with life and all that is).

**Heart Based Practical Exercise
(15 minutes)**

COPY OUT AND COMPLETE IN YOUR JOURNAL THE FOLLOWING STATEMENTS WITH YOUR POSITIVE HEARTFELT ENDINGS

- **I experience love when I.....**
- **When I think about love I feel it in my** (name the area of your body where you feel the energy of love).....
- **I have learnt to love and take care of myself by.....**
- **I have made many changes and the biggest changes I have made for myself are.....**
- **Love fills up so much of my time that I forget to...**
- **I can.....**
- **My heart is full of love because I choose to.....**
- **The inner core of my being recognises love through.....**
- **This is my chance to.....**
- **When I listen to the voice of love it tells me.....**
- **I respect myself totally because.....**
- **I'm determined to.....**
- **I'm so happy that I now choose.....**
- **I am blessed to experience love because.....**
- **I will.....**
- **Love means.....to me**
- **I accept myself, which means.....**
- **I accept love into my life because.....**
- **I have found myself through.....**
- **I am strong enough to.....**
- **Love is now a part of me and I vow to.....**
- **I'm sure.....**
- **I promise to.....**
- **This is my opportunity to.....**
- **It is my mission to.....because.....**
- **I am choosing to make the rest of my life.....**
- **I love myself unconditionally exactly as I am and in doing so I.....**

Remember at any given moment there are a thousand things you can love – David Levitham

CREATING YOUR FUTURE EXACTLY AS YOU WANT IT TO BE

It's time to get familiar with all that the future can hold. There are endless possibilities, and opportunities waiting for you. Life can be amazing and it's never too late to have a happy future.

All relationships begin with you and when you can give to yourself unconditional love and operate from the place of already being completely whole, lovable and deserving then that's what will show up for you in life.

 Turning your 'don't wants to do wants' Heart Based Exercise (10 minutes)

Take some time to reflect on what you are choosing for yourself not just in this moment but for the future. When you choose these things for yourself from your heart, you open up a fountain of endless love and self fulfilment. Turn your don't wants to do wants, doing so will change your energy vibration. The more focused you are on what you want the more likely it will come to you. Focus on what you don't want and you get more of the same!

Don't Wants	Do Wants
I don't want to feel unloved	I want more love
I don't want to attract the wrong kind of partner	I want to attract a loving, considerate and affectionate partner
I don't want a violent or angry partner	I want a partner who can calmly express their feelings
I don't want to feel sad and lonely	I want to be happy and fulfilled

As we come towards the end of the journey back home to you, releasing the power of the past and moving on from self destructive thinking, now will be a great time to redirect your focus to find and keep love.

You have been working through personal limitations and may notice at this point either subtle or dramatic changes in your thinking. You may be feeling different, happier, lighter, more hopeful and optimistic with a sense of curiosity, wonder and excitement for your future and it is my joy to have travelled the journey with you so far.

Every thought you think is, after all, creating your future.

REDIRECT YOUR FOCUS TO FIND AND KEEP LOVE

After working through and releasing the past negative beliefs that have been holding you back from finding you and finding love, this simple exercise of writing down your general positive and empowering beliefs about love and relationships, will show you just how far you've come on this journey of discovery and transformation:

**Practical and EFT Exercise
(20 minutes)**

Complete the following statements in your journal adding at least five additional points below each one.

Speak the statements out loud, or inside your own head, as you tap through your EFT tapping points to increase your positive energy vibration:

- **I love seeing myself...**
  Example: I love seeing myself confident and happy in any situation

- **I love feeling...**
  Example: I love feeling lovable and worthy of love

- **I love hearing...**
  Example: I love hearing the positive voice inside my mind encouraging me to love and accept myself as I am

- **I love knowing...**
  Example: I love knowing that the best is yet to come

- **I am open to...**
  Example: I am open to love

Here is my own definition of love and relationships, having worked through many misunderstandings of what I thought they meant before:

Love is = Loving yourself and knowing that if anyone else can add to that supply of love it is a bonus.

Relationships = The opportunity to be with another as yourself, totally loving accepting yourself first and foremost without the need for another's approval or acceptance.

The wound is the place where the Light enters - Rumi

STANDING IN THE SPOTLIGHT OF LOVE

**Heart Based Exercise
(15 minutes)**

Seeing yourself through the eyes of love every day is a wonderful exercise to practice. The statements below can be completed by either writing them out or speaking them aloud. They will set you up for the day ahead and put you in a positive frame of mind, guiding your thoughts to those which are kind and loving.

- **When I look through the eyes of love, how do I choose to see myself physically today?**

- **When I feel from the heart of love, how can I be more loving to myself today?**

- **When I use my inner wisdom, what thoughts can I choose to think about myself that are more loving?**

- **When I see the love and beauty all around me I start to notice.....**

- **When I focus on all that is possible for me I.....**
- **Today, I realise that when I choose love I.....**
- **Today, tomorrow and the next day I commit to.....**
- **Now and for always I.....**
- **I believe that.....**

 **EFT Practical Exercise
(15 minutes)**

Repeat the following statements out loud as you tap through your points using EFT.

You may wish to tap through the whole list daily, or use one point per day for 5 minutes or so to start and/or end of your day.

- **I accept myself today**
- **I love myself just as I am**
- **I think and speak positively about myself from my heart**
- **I deserve love**
- **I open my heart to love**
- **I attract love easily and effortlessly**
- **I am willing to receive love**
- **I give love with a good heart**
- **I nurture myself and my needs**
- **I choose to do something thoughtful and deserving for myself every day**
- **I am surrounded by love**
- **As I move throughout my day I choose to interact with others from the love that is within me**
- **I seek for the opportunity to notice love in every experience**
- **I am grateful for each loving experience**
- **I choose love in my life every day**
- **I am love**
- **I have found my way back home to me and for that I am truly grateful**

Faith is the bird that feels the light and sings when the dawn is still dark – Rabindranath

ONWARDS AND UPWARDS

I would like to acknowledge you, totally and completely.

I wish to celebrate you and the journey that you have been on so far. It has been the making of you. You may not have previously realised that you have come such a long way in your journey of transformation.

Please take just a moment and reflect on everything you have been through and take a bow in acknowledgement of your lovely self.

Really feel what it feels like to have travelled this far, take a deep breath in, let it out and smile. You are amazing!

There may have been times when you felt like giving up, giving in or worse and I am so very honoured that you are reading this as this is proof that no matter what you've been through, you're still here to tell the tale and that takes courage.

It's time now for you to climb onwards and upwards, stepping into the future that is rightfully yours, towards those things that you are worthy of, to create new beginnings and new opportunities for yourself.

I promise you the best is yet to come, simply follow the techniques offered to you in Find YOU, Find LOVE and the journey home to you will be like no other.

Be aware of the thoughts you are thinking. Separate them from the situation, which is always neutral. It is as it is – Eckhart Tolle

WHAT ELSE IS POSSIBLE?

If you ever wondered whether there was a limit to how happy you can be, how loved and cherished you can feel, how complete you can become - think again, there is no limit, none at all!

COMMITTING TO DOING THE 'INNER WORK'

Whilst writing this book, I have been doing the usual 'inner work' which all EFT Practitioners and therapists are guided to do. Inner work requires us to work through our own limiting beliefs and personal challenges, as well as supporting our clients.

Even as therapists, life still has a way of throwing us setbacks and to be the best that we can be looking after our own needs as well as yours puts us in prime position to guide you to a place of transformation, we too will be walking our talk and tapping alongside you.

Life wasn't designed to be perfect and the only thing that can be perfected is our attitude towards it and our tapping practice as we tap our way through any challenges life throws our way.

MY PERSONAL REFLECTIONS ON LOVE AND LIFE

There were many times when I doubted if it was ok to write this book, as I didn't want to hurt or upset my family with what I was sharing. I felt guilty about the amount of time I spent following my own passions and career aspirations putting my own needs before others. There were times when writing, that I cried as I remembered how low I had become and how close I was to taking my own life in my twenties.

During the writing process, many memories surfaced and I reflected on the times when I witnessed physical violence as a teenager in my mum's second marriage.

I remembered times too; when I thought I was close to dying by the hand of another person who had a difficult relationship with himself. Someone who I loved very much and who was perhaps my greatest teacher as he indirectly taught me to realise what I want and deserve from life.

I have been working through my old memories too as and when they have surfaced while writing this book and applying EFT in the moment.

Transforming the pain from my own past has given me the opportunity to write this book for you.

I want you to know that the more you do the work, the easier it gets. My life has been far from perfect and in many ways it has allowed me to share with you how you too can make the journey back home to yourself.

Using The Spotlight Process along with EFT, you too will transform the things that have hurt you into stepping stones leading you to a brand new future.

IN EACH RELATIONSHIP THERE ARE TWO RELATIONSHIPS, THE ONE YOU HAVE WITH THE OTHER PERSON AND THE ONE YOU HAVE WITH YOURSELF.

I share this very personal poem with you. It's about love being my mission and where that has taken me

Love - Because I wanted it enough

Because I wanted it enough

I moved on from my despair

Because I wanted it enough

I moved on without a care

Because I wanted it enough

I took a risk on being me

Because I wanted it enough

That risk has set me free

Because I wanted it enough

I kept hope along the way

Because I wanted it enough

I took action every day

Because I wanted it enough

I learnt things aren't set in stone

Because I wanted it enough

I found my way back home

Because I wanted it enough

I started loving me

Because I wanted it enough that love has set me free

**Creative Heart Based Exercise
(15 minutes)**

In your journal or on a sheet of paper write a poem or a quote that sums up your own journey. I do believe that by writing this down you will be surprised at just how far you have come.

POSITIVE AND EMPOWERING BELIEFS ABOUT LOVE AND RELATIONSHIPS

We have travelled a long way you and me, thank you for sharing the journey.

You have explored your past; you have taken your skeletons out of the cupboard and had a long overdue spring clean. You have let a lot of emotional baggage go.

Working through the pain from the past isn't easy and you have proved along the way that you are ready to step into the future, the place of hopes and dreams with courage in your heart and faith in yourself that the rest of your life really can be the best of your life.

21 STEPS TO LOVE

I'd like to take you now through a journey of time and space, you set the time frame and I will lead the way. You could take yourself forward in time to one year from this date, three years, five years, ten years whatever time frame jumps out for you, go for that one and follow this simple exercise. You may like to experiment with different time frames, to reveal different sources of information.

Audio Download or Practical Exercise

If you would like to listen to this audio go to the resources section of my website www.wendyfry.com. Additional love and relationship downloads will be added to this page so please keep checking for the recordings that you feel will be supportive to you.

This exercise can be completed by reading it through first and then imagining the outcome of travelling through time and space or via listening to the audio. I am also available to work with you privately for bespoke guided love and relationship sessions in person or over Skype.

Relaxation Exercise (20 minutes)

Find a quiet place to relax, sit back and take three nice deep and easy breaths.

Imagine that you are in your favourite place the place where you truly feel relaxed.

You are enjoying the experience of being comfortable, content and deeply relaxed...

Be aware of your breathing becoming slower and more and more relaxed.

Think about seeing, sensing or imagining that you are travelling forwards in time; you choose the mode of transport and simply sit back and enjoy the ride.

You are willing to go forward to a new time and space in the future and by doing so; your mind will expand and be open to receiving information through your senses, alerting you to all that is possible.

You may also become aware of some changes that you need to make in the here and now, to get you to where you want to be in the future.

Allow your mind to take you where it will.

- Imagine that you have moved beyond your current circumstances forward to your designated time frame (one, three, five or ten years ahead)
- Experience that just for a moment or two
- What have you moved away from?
- What have you moved towards?
- What have you let go off?
- What did you stop doing?
- What did you start doing?
- What are you doing differently now?
- How do you experience your life and love relationships in the future compared to the ones that you are living now?
- What changes have you made between then and now in your life and love relationships that have been positive and beneficial to you?
- Notice your thoughts, how have they changed, what did you have to do to

think differently about love and relationships?

- Notice your feelings now that you have moved on from the past.

- What do you hear going on around you or inside your own head? (This could be your own voice or the voice of others)

- Be aware of any smells or tastes associated with this time frame

- What advice does the 'future you' have to share with you?

- Ask the future you the top three burning questions that you would like information about and find a way of receiving that information for your highest good

- If you took that advice right now and applied it to your life, how would that benefit you?

- If you didn't take that advice what difficulties might remain and how would that limit you?

- Is there anything else that you wish to find out about your future, you may be interested in other life areas outside of love and relationships and the same process can be applied?

- If you have other questions to ask your future self, ask them now, the answers may come through pictures, words or feelings.

- Tune in to the future you carefully, be patient and wait for your answer to come in any way that seems right for you.

- Phrase your questions clearly and in a positive way.

- You may also wish to form questions beginning with who, when, where, why or what before you question your future self

- If this exercise seems a little difficult for you in any way, just pretend that you are able to work through it. Pretend that you are thinking about, seeing, sensing or imagining yourself in the future and it will come.

- What the mind believes it can achieve and 'acting as if' will expand your thinking, your horizons and your measure of love

- Thank your future self for the guidance, knowledge, love and wisdom they share with you, knowing that you can re-connect with them again at any time you wish to

- Bring back with you to your current awareness in this current time and space, the insights and information you have learned from your future self.

- If there were things that were less than you hoped for, ask yourself 'How can I change this for myself?

- What actions do I need to take in order to change this?

- What do I need to stop doing, do differently, or start doing?'

Sometimes, it's about taking action towards what we want in order to bring the changes to us more quickly and effectively. Any information you receive will be for your highest good and will be a guiding light in shaping your future as that all singing, all dancing extravaganza and making your future the best it can be.

Limits exist only in the mind...are you ready to step ever forwards into your future?

This exercise has been adapted with kind permission of Anne Jirsch with excerpts from her Future Life Progression Trainings. Anne is author of The Future Is Yours

YOUR PERSONAL TRANSFORMATION

You now have all the tools you need to Find YOU and Find LOVE. You realise now that the past no longer has a hold on you, and you are free. Free to create your future on your terms exactly as you would like it to be.

 **Insightful Exercise
(15 minutes)**

- **How are you are different now from when you started your journey?**
- **What have you moved on from?**
- **What new and empowering beliefs do you have?**
- **What positive changes have you noticed in your life since reading Find YOU, Find LOVE?**
- **What is your new vision for the future of your love relationships?**

You now have the ability to love yourself unconditionally and from that space your world opens up in so many different ways.

By 'being love' and acting from a loving heart, regardless of what goes on around you, you reliably and consistently find your way back home to you.

Every day you notice subtle changes in your thinking, how you feel and how you show up in the world, you are stronger and more confident than you have ever been. You no longer look back, your new found mission is to focus on the future and all that is possible.

You have your whole life ahead of you and all the love inside of you that you will ever need.

Nothing can dim the light which shines from within – Maya Angelou

**Creative Practical Exercise
(30 minutes)**

THIS IS YOUR LIFE

This is YOUR LIFE and it's time to record your life's events in a positive way, a record in time of how far you have come yourself. It's time to acknowledge your strength, courage, faith and belief in yourself.

I suggest that you purchase a new and very special journal or notebook, something that makes you ooh and ah when you see it and when you touch it, it makes you feel good inside. The colour may inspire you and perhaps it is expensive and of good quality, because after all you're worth it! Some of you may like to make and decorate a beautiful box or photograph album to record just how far you have come or find a special hand crafted container, jewellery box or treasure chest to hold all your wonderful and precious memories, insights and learning. You can decorate your container as you wish, use a multitude of coloured pens, creative items or pleasures, just be sure that it's something very beautiful that makes you feel beautiful when you look at it, feel it and sit with it.

There are several ways you can record your positive time line. You may wish to dooument the positives in your life, by writing them out in a new time line from birth to the present. This will act as a record of happy memories and events, joyful moments, feelings of gratitude and appreciation at different points in your life.

You may choose to collect pictures from birth to now of happy memories and fill the pages with mementoes to record significant events, wonderful experiences, opportunities and triumphs. You may decide to make notes, write a letter and write a poem or a story of thanks to the people in your life alive or deceased, who have supported you, encouraged you and been there for you along the way.

You may consider asking family members, friends and acquaintances to write a piece for your project about the difference you have made to them, the things they love about you, their words of love, care and appreciation.

You can collect and add to your project any items that make you feel good. I have known my clients to add glitter, little trinkets from nature, photographs, pictures they have drawn, inspiring quotations, and words of affirmation from their nearest and dearest.

You can also make recordings of your friends and family talking to you about your life and achievements to date and you can also record your time line like this if you wish to, perhaps with some inspiring and energising music running in the background.

It's a wonderful exercise to do, as you will be focusing on the positive aspects of your life and just how far you have come.

When you focus on all the good in your life, all the special things to appreciate in the moment, your gratitude and positivity become a guiding force for the future. You look through new eyes towards what else is possible for you, what else can be achieved.

By completing this exercise, your focus is on gratitude and aligned with what you want from life. You focus from the highest point of vibration, attracting to you positive people and positive circumstances.

By finding you, you find love, the love that you had inside of you all along.

NAMASTE

♥

I honour the place in you where the entire universe resides. A place of light, love, truth, peace and wisdom. I honour the place in you where, when you are in that place, and I am in that place, there is only one of us.

Mohandas Gandhi

APPENDIX

AFTER CARE AND SUPPORT:

You have already taken transformational steps in finding you and finding love. If you are wondering what to do next to fully implement the learning, take a moment and consider the following options:

- You may wish to work with me on a programme of support privately to further the progress you have already made, see my website www.wendyfry.com
- Download the free resources and audios on my website www.wendyfry.com/resources
- Attend one of my workshops
- Connect on my You Tube Channel
- Connect with me and others readers on my Facebook Find YOU, Find LOVE page
- Connect with me on Twitter via my website
- Sign up to my newsletter via my website
- Follow my blog via my website
- Leave a book review on www.amazon.co.uk or contact me direct with your feedback
- Share the love and give the gift of this book to others who you feel will benefit
- Let others know that they are lovable through word, thought and deed
- Use The Spotlight Process and EFT daily in your life
- Practice daily gratitude, giving thanks for all that you have

Research Articles: United Nations Convention on the Rights of the Child. Distr. General CRC/C/GC/7 Rev.1. 20 September 2006

RESOURCES

- **Gary Craig** www.emofree.com for additional information about EFT and free EFT manual for further study
- **Karl Dawson** www.efttrainingcourses.net for forthcoming training courses and information about EFT and Matrix Reimprinting
- **The AMT** www.TheAMT.com The Association for Meridian & Energy Therapies, home of Energy EFT, Positive EFT & Energy In Motion (EmoTrance)

- **Silvia Hartmann** www.silviahartmann.com Creator of Positive EFT and Energy In Motion (EmoTrance)

- **EFT Universe** www.eftuniverse.com/research-and-studies/research is a great resource aid for all things EFT including research and resources of all kinds

- **Curly Martin** www.achievementspecialists.co.uk Curly is in my opinion one of the best coaches on the planet, check out her training courses and range of bestselling books on coaching

- **Sasha Allenby** www.sashaallenby.com Sasha has been a key player in helping me to write Find YOU, Find LOVE, if you need any support of this kind consider her 'Write a Book in 12 weeks' programme

- **Dr. Peter Kavanagh** www.healingspiritwithin.co.uk Complementary Therapist & Soul Plan Practitioner & Teacher. Peter's Soul Plan Reading confirmed that I'm on the right path in terms of doing the work I love in service to others and that writing is indeed part of my future.

- **Anne Jirsch** www.annejirsch.com   Anne is one of the world's leading experts and pioneers of Future Life Progression. Bestselling Author of Instant Intuition, The Future is Yours, Cosmic Energy, Create Your Perfect Future.

- **Kate Marillat** www.katemarillat.com Creativity Coach and Author of Transform Your Beliefs, Transform Your Life. Kate inspired me to write Find YOU, Find LOVE, it was through her guidance to tap into the creative part of myself that got me into the flow of writing

- **Sharon King** www.magicalnewbeginnings.com Author of The Missing Peace - A new Paradigm in Conscious Birthing. Sharon offers a range of training courses and workshops including Matrix Birth Reimprinting, Colour Mirrors and Mind Calm Meditation.

- **Caroline Maidment** www.tranquility-music.co.uk offers a range of meditation CD's and is also an EFT Practitioner and Hypnotherapist who I have worked with personally www.loveyourlifetherapy.com

If you are considering writing your own book I recommend personal coaching and mentoring with:

- **Kate Marillat:** Creativity Coach and Author of Transform Your Beliefs, Transform Your Life www.katemarillat.com.

- **Sasha Allenby:** www.sashaallenby.com Author of Write an Evolutionary Self Help Book – The Definitive Guide for Spiritual Entrepreneurs. Sasha offers a range of coaching and mentoring programmes

- **Richard McMunn:** http://www.bookpublishingacademy.co.uk (one to one coaching option with Richard McMunn) this is a must have for the publishing and marketing aspect of writing.

If you have enjoyed the illustrations in Find YOU, Find LOVE

- **Amy Branton** shares her illustrations on
  http://www.pinterest.com/freehearteft/living-from-the-heart/
  Amy is also a skilled EFT and Matrix Reimprinting Practitioner
  www.freehearteft.co.uk

For additional enjoyment and reading I recommend the following books:

- Boyes, Carolyn. Need to know? NLP – Achieve success with positive thinking. Collins, London, UK. 2006
- Cava, Roberta. Dealing with Difficult People, Proven strategies for handling stressful situations and defusing tensions. Judy Piatakus Ltd, London, UK. 1990
- Chapman, Gary. The Five Love Languages for Singles. Northfield Publishing, Chicago, Illinois. 2004
- Childare, Doc & Martin, Howard. The HeartMath Solution: The Institute of HeartMath's Revolutionary Program for Engaging the Power of the heart's Intelligence. Harper Collins. USA. 1999
- Craig, Gary. The EFT Manual. Energy Psychology Press. Santa Rosa, California. 2010,2011
- Dawson, Karl. Marillat, Kate. Transform Your Beliefs, Transform Your Life. EFT Tapping using Matrix Reimprinting. Hay House, London, UK. 2014
- Dawson, Karl. Allenby, Sasha. Matrix Reimprinting using EFT. Hay House, London, UK. 2010
- Dodd, Ray. The Power of Belief. Hampton Road Publishing Company, Inc. Charlottesville, Virginia. 2003
- Hartmann, Silvia. Positive EFT. DragonRising, United Kingdom. 2013. To find out more about Positive EFT and The SUE Scale
- Holden, Robert. Loveability. Hay House, London UK. 2013
- Jirsch, Anne. Cafferky, Monica. The Future is Yours. Piatikus. Great Britian. 2007
- Katie, Byron. Loving What Is. Random House. USA. 2002
- Lipton, Bruce. Spontaneous Evolution: Our Positive Future and a Way to Get There from Here. Hay House, UK. 2009
- Losier, Michael. Law of Attraction. Michael J. Losier Enterprises Inc. Canada. 2006
- Martin, Curly. The Life Coaching Handbook. Crown House Publishing Ltd. Wales, UK. 2001
- McKay, Matthew, PhD. Fanning, Patrick. Prisoners of Belief. New Harbinger Publications, Inc. Oakland, California. 1991
- Scare, Dr Robert. The Body Bears the Burden: Trauma, Dissociation and Disease, Haworth Medical Press, second edition. 2007

ABOUT THE AUTHOR

Wendy first became interested in emotional health and wellbeing after overcoming many challenges in her personal life. Through exploring her past, changing her limiting beliefs and working through her own demons, Wendy has gone on to train extensively to support you as you transform your own love and relationship problems.

Wendy reaches out from her heart to yours through the contents of this book in the hope that she can support you to turn around any limiting beliefs that you may have about love and relationships. It's the choices that you take from now on that will ultimately lift you up or keep you down. Read on through the entirety of this book and then decide if staying stay stuck where you are has any benefit. Will you let the past dictate the future, or will you take responsibility for the rest of your life to be the best of your life?

Wendy offers support and guidance through a range of healing modalities: EFT (Emotional Freedom Technique), Matrix Reimprinting, Hypnotherapy, Life Coaching, NLP (Neuro Linguistic Programming) Picture Tapping Technique, Energy In Motion (Emo Trance), Matrix Birth Reimprinting, Future Life Progression and Positive EFT.

Wendy is a member of The British Institute of Hypnotherapists (BIH), Registered with the International Coaching Institute of Coaching and Mentoring (IIC&M), member of The Association of Energy Meridian Therapists (AMT) and The Association for the Advancement of Meridian Energy Techniques (AAMET)

Wendy has a practice based in Surrey, United Kingdom and she also works internationally over Skype and running workshops worldwide.